M^cCARTHYISM

Third Edition

M^cCARTHYISM

Edited by Thomas C. Reeves
The University of Wisconsin—Parkside

Third Edition

KRIEGER PUBLISHING COMPANY
MALABAR, FLORIDA

Third Edition 1989

Printed and Published by
Robert E. Krieger Publishing Company, Inc.
Krieger Drive
Malabar, FL 32950

Printed in the United States of America

Library of Congress Cataloging-in-Publication Data

McCarthyism / edited by Thomas C. Reeves. — 3rd ed.
    p.   cm.
  Bibliography: p.
  ISBN 0-89464-289-8 (alk. paper)
  1. Internal security—United States—History—20th century.
2. McCarthy, Joseph, 1908–1957.   3. Communism—United States—1917–
4. Subversive activities—United States—History—20th century.
5. Anti-communist movements—United States—History—20th century.
I. Reeves, Thomas C., 1936–
E743.5.M37   1989
322.4'2—dc19   88-13666
10 9 8 7 6 5 4 3

Contents

CORNERED.

Source: *New York Times* March 26, 1950 ©1950 by New York Times Company.
Reprinted by permission.

Introduction

From early 1950, when he first vaulted onto the front pages, through late 1954, when he was condemned by the United States Senate, few Americans attracted so much attention as Senator Joseph R. McCarthy of Wisconsin. His dramatic and much-publicized attacks against what he called Communist subversion in the federal government struck some people as a heroic crusade designed to save the United States from treason at home and failure abroad. Many saw in his charges a convincing explanation of what had "gone wrong" in America since the Second World War. He won the favor of millions. In January 1954 a Gallup Poll indicated that 50 percent of the American people had a generally "favorable opinion" of him. Later that year, facing Senate censure, a Committee of Ten Million Mobilizing for Justice delivered a supporting petition to the Capitol said to bear the names of 1,000,816 McCarthy admirers. He consistently won praise from the powerful Hearst and Scripps-Howard newspapers, as well as from the widely read *Chicago Tribune*, *Washington Times-Herald*, and *New York Daily News*. The American Legion and the Daughters of the American Revolution lauded his patriotism. Such popular radio commentators as Fulton Lewis, Jr., Walter Winchell, and Paul Harvey championed his allegations. Vice-President Richard Nixon and Senators Everett Dirksen, Karl Mundt, James Eastland, Barry Goldwater, William Knowland, William Jenner, and Pat McCarran were considered among his close friends and advisers. Congressional and state investigating committees often applauded his efforts. The Republican party found McCarthy one of its most sought-after speakers, and he frequently toured the country on behalf of G.O.P. candidates. In 1952 the Senator addressed his party's National Convention. Nixon was placed on the presidential ticket that year to placate the McCarthyite wing of the G.O.P.

In mid-1953, Federal Bureau of Investigation Director J. Edgar Hoover, one of the most respected and admired men in America, told reporters, "I've come to know Senator McCarthy well, officially and personally. I view him as a friend and I believe he so views me. Certainly, he is a controversial man. He is earnest and he is honest. He has enemies. Whenever you attack subversives of any kind, Communists, Fascists, even the Ku Klux Klan, you are going to be the victim of the most extremely vicious criticism that can be made."

But to others Joe (as he always referred to himself) McCarthy was a ruthless and irresponsible political opportunist, a demagogue, a totalitarian, perhaps even a fascist. He generated as much fear and loathing in this country and overseas as any American ever has. His tactics drew heated—often shrill—criticism from within the intellectual community (to this day not a single major textbook on American history speaks kindly of him), and the nation's most prestigious newspapers and magazines bitterly opposed him. To many he became a symbol of an impending mass conformity, of the suppression of the Bill of Rights, even of the demose of democracy. McCarthy's critics labeled the 1950s "The Age of Fear," "The Era of Anxiety," and "The Nightmare Decade," and the focus of that view was invariably the Senator himself.

"McCarthyism" was a term coined in late March 1953 by *Washington Post* cartoonist Herbert Block (Herblock) to describe McCarthy's reckless behavior: his practice of smearing innocent people with a Red brush for his own, usually political, purposes. But to many scholars the word properly transcends the activities of a single man. Why, after all, should one senator have mattered that much? His talents and faults had been equaled by other politicians without evoking the sort of passions that surrounded his name. It is now clear that what historians call the "Second Red Scare" preceded McCarthy's assault upon the State Department by at least a year and a half and retained its vigor beyond his condemnation by the Senate by perhaps as much as three years. Its effects may be seen in the Congress, and in courts, churches, schools, press, libraries, the entertainment industry, and state and local governments of the time. Long-range political explanations have been posited. Sociological, psychological, even economic roots of the phenomenon have been explored. Activities of a variety of citizens, including President Ronald Reagan, have stimulated frequent warnings of a "New McCarthyism."

Clearly, McCarthy and McCarthyism rose to prominence at a time when large numbers of Americans were shocked and frustrated by the course of current events. The lofty goals they had associated with the conclusion of a bloody and costly war seemed cruelly overshadowed by news of Communist subversion and triumph. How was one to explain the discovery in 1945 of over a thousand classified government documents in the offices of the left-wing magazine *Amerasia*? The following year, in Canada, several Soviet spy rings that had sent atomic secrets and uranium samples to Moscow were uncovered. In 1947 the House Committee on Un-American Activities claimed that Americans were being brain-washed by Reds in the motion picture industry. In August 1948 testimony before that same Committee linked scores of prominent Americans with Soviet espionage, including a one-time assistant to President Roosevelt, a former Assistant Secretary of the Treasury, and Alger Hiss, a former State Department official and current head of the Carnegie Endowment for International Peace. Hiss sued the informant, Whittaker Chambers, formerly a Soviet agent and later a senior editor for *Time*, and the charges and countercharges flying between the two dominated hedlines for a year and a half. The dimensions of the confrontation superseded the immediate facts: President Truman, Secretary of State Dean Acheson, Adlai Stevenson, and a large number of others of liberal persuasion expressed support for Hiss, while those who professed to believe that the New Deal and the Democratic party were infected with Communism loudly defended Chambers. The matter concluded with Hiss's conviction for perjury—in part for telling a grand jury under oath that he had not passed secret documents to Chambers in the 1930s—and many Americans became convinced that the Roosevelt and Truman administrations had been, at best, oblivious to the dangers of internal Communist subversion.

"The shocks of 1949," Eric Goldman later commented, "loosed within American life a vast impatience, a turbulent bitterness, a rancor akin to revolt. It was a strange rebelliousness, quite without parallel in the history of the United States." Part of this stemmed from the Hiss trials. Americans were stunned when Judith Coplon, a Justice Department employee, was arrested and convicted for passing secrets to a Soviet agent. They were also deeply disturbed by news of China's fall to Communists. Highly respected Senator Robert Taft of Ohio and other Republican leaders charged that the loss was directly related to treason and appeasement within the federal government. And in September of that year President Truman sadly announced that the Soviet Union possessed—somehow—the atomic bomb.

On February 3, 1950, less than two weeks after Hiss's conviction, the British government released the story of the arrest and confession of Dr. Klaus Fuchs, a physicist who had worked at Los Alamos during the war and had delivered vital atomic information to the Russians. (His testimony was to lead to the conviction and execution of Julius and Ethel Rosenberg as Soviet spies.) Six days later Joe McCarthy flew to Wheeling, West Virginia and told a Republican rally that he possessed the names of Communists at work in the State Department—205 of them!

As the selection by Daniel Bell points out, it is ironic that the national anxiety over Communists occurred at a time when the Communist party in the United States was virtually impotent. Nevertheless, the spy cases and Republican charges helped prompt the Truman Administration to wage an intensive drive against Communist espionage and infiltration. In March 1947 the President issued an Executive Order creating a new loyalty program for the federal government and requesting an investigation of all federal employees by the FBI and the Civil Service Commission. The following year the Department of Justice obtained the indictment of eleven leaders of the American Communist Party for violating the Smith Act of 1940—for conspiring to *teach and advocate* the violent overthrow of the United States. After a long and stormy trial the Communists were convicted, and on appeal the Smith Act was declared constitutional by the Supreme Court. The Justice Department then won convictions against some forty additional Communist leaders. Congress responded to the tempo by passing the McCarran Act of 1950, the severest internal security bill since the Sedition Act of 1918. But to Joe McCarthy and his friends all such efforts were grossly inadequate.

After his Wheeling speech, McCarthy made one sensational allegation after another. He called Foreign Service officer John Stewart Service "a known associate and collaborator with Communists and pro-Communists." He said that Ambassador At Large Philip C. Jessup had an "unusual affinity" for Communist causes. Dr. Owen Lattimore of The Johns Hopkins University, a respected Far East scholar, was called "the top Russian espionage agent in the country." In 1951 McCarthy contended that General George C. Marshall was part of "a conspiracy so immense and an infamy so black as to dwarf any previous such venture in the history of man." At the Republican National Convention in 1952 and throughout the campaign to elect Eisenhower and Nixon (and reelect himself), McCarthy hammered away at Democrats ("Commiecrats") for their "softness" on Communism. In victory, he continued his assault. In 1953 he charged that Harry Truman had knowingly appointed a Soviet agent to the International Monetary Fund. As Chairman of the Permanent Subcommittee on Investigations of the Senate Government Operations Committee, he conducted widely publicized hearings into subversion in the Voice of America, the State Department's overseas information programs, and in the Army Signal Center at Fort Monmouth, New Jersey. (Unidentified government employees leaked secret documents to the Senator, as did active and former FBI officials.) He challenged the Eisenhower Administration's appointment of Charles Bohlen as ambassador to the Soviet Union. He brazenly made a private agreement with Greek shipowners concerning trade with Red China, and threatened to investigate the Central Intelligence Agency, headed by Allen Dulles, the Secretary of State's brother.

By early 1954 McCarthy had reached the peak of his power, feeling free to blast the Democratic party for "twenty years of treason" and to take cracks at leaders of his own party for failing to heed fully his advice. The Eisenhower Administration finally broke with McCarthy in February over his attacks on the U.S. Army. The encounter stemmed from the drafting of McCarthy aide G. David Schine and the subsequent rage of his close friend Roy Cohn, another young McCarthy assistant. The clash led to 36 days of nationally televised hearings during which millions watched McCarthy's tactics. The famed Army-McCarthy hearings destroyed the senator's national popularity and led to his downfall.

On July 30 a resolution was introduced in the Senate by Republican rebel Ralph Flanders of Vermont to censure McCarthy for an assortment of offenses against the Senate and its members. After an investigation headed by Republican Senator Arthur Watkins of Utah (and after the November elections) the Senate voted 67-22 to condemn. Joe McCarthy was the fourth senator in American history to be so chastised by his colleagues.

From that point on, the fight went out of McCarthy. He continued, almost halfheartedly, to rail against "pinks" and Reds, but almost no one paid any attention. Many senators snubbed him. The press, which in its eagerness for headlines had helped make him famous, now boycotted his press conferences and ignored his press releases. The Eisenhowers let it be known that McCarthy was the only senator unwelcome at the White House. Saddened by the rebukes and plagued by alcoholism, a problem of several years' duration, McCarthy died of a liver ailment in May 1957 at the age of 48.

Joe McCarthy, the man and his methods, is the subject of the opening section of this book. The editor examines McCarthy's formative years, education, and early political career, and attempts to provide insights into his complex and little understood psychological makeup. Richard Fried examines McCarthy's rendezvous with the Anti-communist issue and describes a famous Senate speech. James Wechsler, a liberal journalist, gives an account of his confrontation with Senator McCarthy in 1953. To Wechsler, McCarthy was a calculating, cynical demagogue whose "brute brilliance" fascinated even his victims.

On the other hand, conservatives William F. Buckley, Jr. and L. Brent Bozell portray McCarthy as an effective Anti-communist whose "interpretations" of facts called the nation's attention to an insidious domestic menace. McCarthy employee Roy Cohn evaluates the senator's "broad brush techniques" and concludes that McCarthy, despite his exaggerations and crudities, was a "courageous man who fought a monumental evil.

How can McCarthy's methods be fairly judged? Were exaggeration and bombast necessary? How far from solid facts did the senator stray? What, if any, were his long-range goals?

As previously noted, many scholars think that too much emphasis has been placed on McCarthy's brief political career and stress the fact that McCarthyism was a broader political phenomenon. The second section of this book deals with McCarthyism and partisan politics. Athan Theoharis claims that the Truman Administration had much to do with the rise of McCarthyism because of its hardline approach toward Russia and its penchant for overemphasizing the presence of Communist espionage in the federal bureaucracy. President Truman actually contributed to passage of the McCarran Act, Theoharis maintains, due to his willingness to concede some of the misconceptions on which the Red Scare was constructed.

Earl Latham takes the position that McCarthyism was prompted by the Republican party's wholly unexpected and enraging defeat in the presidential contest of 1948. By wielding the expedient issue of Communist infiltration, conservative Republicans, with the help of some southern Democrats, gained control of Congress in 1950. They then found a useful instrument in Joe McCarthy and intensified their drive against "internal subversion" with an eye to the elections of 1952. In short, McCarthyism was a right-wing tool for winning elections by smearing political opponents.

Richard Rovere contends, in contrast, that McCarthyism was a "bipartisan doctrine," with strong support among Democratic party leaders and voters. Does he illustrate this point satisfactorily? Is it important to note that not a single Democrat voted against McCarthy's condemnation? How can one account for the fear McCarthy stirred in both Democratic and Republican administrations.?

George Kennan sees little difference between the Democratic and Republican approaches to the pursuit of subversives in the federal government. Why was so much fuss made about John Paton Davies, Jr.? Could one minor official have misdirected an entire foreign policy?

Ellen Schrecker, in describing the Red Scare in higher education, thinks that liberals were just as guilty as conservatives in perpetuating the hysteria. "Every segment of society was involved," she claims, not least of all the academic establishment. May one generalize so broadly about the thousands of men and women who teach and administer in America's colleges and universities? Do academics ever have the power, as Schrecker claims, to direct the intellectual tone of the entire nation for an extended period of time?

Some scholars have seen even broader issues in the general topic. During the peak of McCarthy's career a number of prominent social scientists linked McCarthyism with pre-New Deal agrarian radicalism. They argued that the Wisconsin senator drew powerful support from areas in which Populism and Progressivism had been strong and from groups long known for their hatred of cities, Jews, and blacks, their isolation and fear of big government, and their distrust of authority and expert knowledge. These "pluralists," as the scholars would be labeled, saw McCarthy's attacks against Ivy League colleges and universities, intellectuals, and smooth-talking pin-striped diplomats as examples of agrarian demagoguery. The Communism in government issue was a guise for a rebellion against the Eastern establishment; McCarthy was a radical democrat. In the section on McCarthyism and mass movements, Peter Viereck represents the furthest extreme of this position, contending that McCarthyism was "Populism gone sour." Especially interesting is his point that McCarthy drove many liberals toward a sort of neo-conservatism, compelling them to lose faith in the masses they had championed during the Depression.

Other pluralists adopted portions of this view to explain McCarthyism as an expression of "status strains" within American society. In times of rapid change and prosperity, the argument ran, when attention is turned away from economic needs, the anxieties of social groups rising and falling in status often prompt them to turn to politics as a channel for their frustrations. Joe McCarthy's "peculiar power," wrote Seymour Martin Lipset, was that to "the status-deprived he is a critic of the upper class; to the privileged, he is a foe of social change and Communism." The selection by Daniel Bell stresses the congruence of Populism and status anxieties within the political framework of the postwar years and eloquently portrays the American penchant for moralizing.

Several questions might be raised about the "status strains" interpretation. Aren't status anxieties present at all times in a relatively classless society? Are those losing status always aware of their decline in social rank when they enter the polling booth? And why doesn't a species of McCarthyism appear in all prosperous eras? (In fact, the Alien and Sedition Acts and the Palmer raids of the Wilson administration, two outbursts of intolerance similar to McCarthyism, occurred when the nation's economy was in a slump.)

Michael Paul Rogin studied voting behavior in Wisconsin and the Dakotas and found that McCarthyism was closely related to conservative Republican politics, thus returning our attention to the political aims of McCarthyites. In his selection Rogin contends that McCarthyism and agrarian radicalism had nothing in common and that pluralist conclusions were grounded on a mistrust of the common man and direct democracy.

Seymour Martin Lipset and Earl Raab, in a book published in 1970, attempted a synthesis of views about McCarthyism. To them it was an apolitical tendency of the early 1950s centered on America's fear and hatred of Communism. Nevertheless, the authors add, several groups supported McCarthy for reasons unrelated to anticommunism—reasons that should remind us of the pluralist arguments. Is this well-written blend of positions convincing? Is McCarthyism fully explained? How can one reconcile "For McCarthyism, the enemy was an ideology, Communism" and "McCarthy's main targets were never the North Korean or Chinese or Russian Communists—not even seriously, Communist spies in America—but rather the American establishment"?

These varied views of McCarthyism are presented in the hope that students will be less inclined to select the "right one" than to think about and discuss the dimensions of one of the more controversial phenomena of recent American history. The existence of complexity is one of the highest lessons of higher education. It is equally useful to ponder the variety of conclusions men and women of learning and integrity may derive from essentially the same evidence, and to gauge the polemics of those who seek to plead a case rather than prove it. Along the way, one hopes, students will also learn something of the tension-filled period between the dropping of the atomic bombs and the launching of Sputnik, for in those years lie some valuable truths about the character and collective mentality of the American people.

Part One

JOSEPH R. McCARTHY: THE MAN AND HIS METHODS

Chapter 1   JOE: THE YEARS BEFORE WHEELING

The editor, THOMAS C. REEVES (b. 1936), has written extensively on the post-war years. The following selection, written especially for this volume, is based on his book *The Life and Times of Joe McCarthy*, published in 1982. What elements of the Senator's earlier life help us to understand the motives behind the speech at Wheeling, West Virginia?

Joseph Raymond McCarthy was born in 1908, the fifth child of Timothy and Bridget McCarthy. The McCarthys operated a 142-acre farm about seven miles northwest of Appleton, Wisconsin, and seemed to their neighbors to be a perfectly average couple: hard-working, friendly, devoutly Roman Catholic, and deeply devoted to each other and their children. Six of the seven McCarthy children were to lead normal, uneventful lives in the area. Joe, as he was always called, was exceptional from the start.

He was an almost totally extroverted youngster: loud, fun-loving, self-confident, aggressive, and daring. He was extremely popular; wherever he was, a sister later recalled, there was a crowd. Joe was also hyperactive and capable of feats of sustained labor that amazed others. His very high intelligence was recognized early, and he breezed through the local elementary school a year ahead of most of his peers.

After a few years as a farm hand and chicken rancher, Joe took a job with a local grocery store chain and soon returned to school in the nearby town of

Manawa. Working with a passion that astounded his teachers and fellow students, he completed four years of high school courses in nine months, earning top grades. He somehow also found time to be active in school affairs and keep up a daily routine of rigorous physical exercise. Everyone in town liked and admired Joe McCarthy.

In 1930 he entered Marquette University, a Jesuit institution in Milwaukee. For two years he enrolled in pre-engineering courses. Influenced by friends, he switched to the law school and took the normal three years to complete his degree. Now in his mid-twenties and surrounded by the pleasures of a large city, Joe took a much more casual approach to his studies. He depended upon his highly retentive memory, last-minute cramming sessions with the studious, and a certain amount of bluffing to get through his classes. Most of his energy was devoted to off-campus employment, poker games and parties at a law school fraternity, and an assortment of campus activities including a stint as boxing coach. Joe was one of the most popular students at Marquette and earned a considerable reputation as a ladies' man. (Later attempts by political opponents to portray him as a homosexual were greeted with laughter by those who knew him best.) This lack of serious intellectual preparation and a deep-seated reliance upon hasty memorization and bluffing would have serious consequences for McCarthy in the future.

In 1935 Joe opened a private law practice in Waupaca, a small county seat not far from Appleton. He had few clients and made little money. Much of his time was spent making friends, playing poker, and dating attractive young women. Nine months later he was hired by Mike G. Eberlein, an established attorney in Shawano, forty-five miles away. Eberlein provided his young friend with a regular salary and some valuable experience in the court room.

In Shawano Joe began to have political aspirations. He became president of the Young Democratic Clubs of the Seventh District (the McCarthys had traditionally been Democrats), and in 1936 he ran unsuccessfully for district attorney. During the campaign he won attention for his vituperative rhetoric, and he greatly irritated the incumbent by publishing a pamphlet noting his minor violation of a local ordinance. Others were greatly attracted to the robust, good-looking young candidate because of his sunny personality, his extreme (and wholly sincere) generosity, especially toward children, and his ability to remember the name of almost everyone he met.

Three years later McCarthy entered the race for circuit judge. He was almost alone in thinking he could defeat the incumbent, sixty-six-year-old Edgar V. Werner, a judge for more than twenty years. "Watch me," he told a friend, "I'll go door to door." Joe borrowed money from friends, purchased a new car, and began to visit farmhouses and small towns fourteen and more hours a day, shaking hands, slapping backs, buying drinks, swapping stories, and asking for votes. With the aid of scores of friends, he sent what appeared to be a personally handwritten postcard to every voter in the tenth judicial circuit region requesting support. He also attacked Werner personally, in speeches and in advertisements, making the judge seem older and wealthier than he actually was. One observer, who knew McCarthy well, thought him "tricky, very tricky." In April 1939, Joe won the election by a narrow margin, becoming the youngest man ever to be elected a circuit judge in Wisconsin.

On the whole, McCarthy was a good judge. He acted in haste at times, and in 1941 received a sharply worded rebuke from the chief justice of the State Supreme Court for destroying court notes in a case. But he worked extremely hard, was consistently fair, and won the admiration of virtually all of the local attorneys.

Joe was not on the bench long before he confided to friends that he was going to run for the United States Senate. He began to race all over the state, filling in for judges who were ill or on vacation. These opportunities enabled him to make hundreds of new friends—and future campaign workers. For all of his energy, however, it seemed most unlikely that McCarthy could ever muster enough support to oust either of the powerful incumbents, Republican Alexander Wiley and Progressive Robert La Follette, Jr. He had little money, virtually no knowledge of national or international issues, and was still a Democrat in a highly Republican state. Joe ignored the odds; his victory, he told confidants, was simply a matter of time.

The war temporarily interrupted McCarthy's plans. In mid-1942 he joined the Marine Corps and not long afterward found himself in the South Pacific as an intelligence officer for a dive-bomber squadron. Even at this distance from home, however, Joe's thoughts soon turned toward his political future. Having suffered a broken bone in his left foot during a "shellback" ceremony accident aboard ship, he had friendly newsmen send stories to Wisconsin stating that he had been wounded in action. He then forged—or had someone else forge—his commanding officer's signature to a document that won him a citation from Admiral Nimitz describing his heroism. The press releases and the citation, he knew, would be effective campaign advertisements one day. (After the war he would occasionally fake a limp on the campaign trail, telling audiences that he had ten pounds of shrapnel in his left leg.)

Joe also made eleven flights in the squadron's two-man dive-bombers. He greatly enjoyed firing the machine guns, and saw some slight action during a couple of flights. His major reason for wangling these assignments, however, was political. He had photographs taken of himself in the gunner's seat and would soon refer to himself as "Tailgunner Joe." In each of his subsequent campaigns he would inflate the number of flights he went on during the war to stress his valor in combat. (By 1952 the total became 32, and the Marine Corps awarded him the Distinguished Flying Cross.)

In 1944, while still in the South Pacific, McCarthy declared himself a

Republican and entered the primary race against Senator Wiley. The campaign was secretly financed by an unusually fortunate railroad investment made just before Joe entered the service. (He was to claim falsely that close relatives provided him with the bulk of his campaign expenses.) He hired a small staff which opened a campaign office in Appleton, prepared 2½ million pieces of literature stressing their candidate's military heroism, and produced an assortment of banners, signs, and newspaper advertisements. Joe took a fifteen-day leave in Wisconsin, displaying his colorful uniform, showing reporters the Nimitz citation, and delivering a few platitude-filled speeches. While overseas he buttonholed troops from Wisconsin, put signs on two trucks and a jeep reading MCCARTHY FOR U.S. SENATOR, and painted HEADQUARTERS, MCCARTHY FOR U.S. SENATOR across his tent. He continued to inspire dramatic press releases for Wisconsin consumption. One glorified his role as an intelligence officer:

Every evening "the judge" holds court in a dilapidated shack just off a jungle air strip deep in the South Pacific combat zone.

The folks back in Wisconsin might be a trifle shocked at his lack of dignity now. He stands barechested before his bench, an ancient table reeling on its last legs, and opens court with:

"All right, what kind of hell did you give the Japs today?"

McCarthy did surprisingly well in the election, placing second and garnering almost 80,000 votes. He solidly carried the counties within his judicial district and came close to winning seven other counties. Joe was elated by the outcome and looked forward to running again when the next opportunity arose.

In December 1944, McCarthy resigned from the Marine Corps. He attributed his departure publicly to his "war wound," but he actually left the service to campaign for reelection as judge. Winning the election in April without opposition, Joe immediately began to lay plans for the 1946 race against Senator La Follette.

Throughout the remainder of 1945 McCarthy crisscrossed the state with a fury, making public appearances, giving speeches, and enlisting supporters. He forged close ties with leaders of the newly recreated Young Republican organization. They were especially helpful in wooing senior G.O.P. officials, who were suspicious of McCarthy's Democratic past and initially put off by his youth, inexperience, and somewhat rustic social graces.

The guiding force of the state Republicans was conservative Madison industrialist Thomas E. Coleman, a long-time archenemy of Robert La Follette, Jr. When the Senator announced his return to the G.O.P. in March 1946 from the defunct Progressive Party (the liberal Progressives had departed in 1934 to become allies of the New Deal), Coleman became desperate to find a candidate capable of defeating him in the primary. No one had collected nearly as much support as the perpetually campaigning judge from Appleton. Reluctantly, Coleman gave in to pleas from the Young Republicans and pledged his support for McCarthy. There seemed to be no alternative, and he would do anything to defeat La Follette.

In early May Joe won the endorsement of the Republican Voluntary Committee, the inner circle of the state G.O.P. He made only a single vow in his acceptance speech: "I don't claim to be more brilliant than the next man, but I have always claimed that I have worked harder. I am going to work harder. That's a promise." Most observers were extremely doubtful that energy, hard work, and even access to Republican coffers would enable McCarthy to topple "Fighting Bob" La Follette's popular son, a prominent voice in the Senate since 1925. Joe entered the battle a decided underdog.

The McCarthy campaign was perhaps the most active in state history. Hundreds of volunteers worked tirelessly on his behalf, supervising the dispatch of a "personalized" postcard to every voter in the state, raising funds, organizing rallies, planning and distributing campaign literature, making speeches, and knocking on doors. Harold Townsend, a wealthy Milwaukee construction executive, was one of several key supporters who took leaves from their jobs to work full-time for McCarthy. One long-time confidant, Otis Gomillion of Milwaukee, traveled 33,000 miles with the candidate by the end of the summer and wore out two automobiles in the process. Almost all of the volunteers were attracted to the campaign by Joe McCarthy's personality. Young Republican leader Lloyd Tegge of Waukesha said later, "It was a personal thing." When you really got to know Joe, "He became part of your family."

As promised, McCarthy labored at a breakneck pace between his nomination and the August 13 election. Fourteen-hour days of non-stop campaigning were common. In one four-day period he made appearances in twenty-seven cities and towns. Somehow he managed to continue his judicial duties without interruption.

Joe's speeches contained little of substance. They stressed his war record and featured standard Republican charges about big government, corruption, and high taxes. His expensive campaign literature and advertisements featured a number of wartime photographs and avoided virtually any reference to significant issues. As the primary neared, Joe lashed out at La Follette over alleged conflicts of interest. He also condemned the Senator's isolationist voting record, which he said in one speech played "into the hands of the Communists." Joe's public challenge to debate was met with lofty silence.

La Follette, an ill, moody man who detested campaigning, chose to work in his Washington office until a week before the election. His attitude toward reelection was strangely ambivalent. What efforts he made on his behalf were largely ineffective. He found himself under attack not only by McCarthy but by Democratic candidate Howard J. McMurray, who had strong labor support and claimed backing by President Roosevelt. Communist leaders within the C.I.O. also attacked La Follette because of his hostile attitude toward the Soviet Union.

McCarthy shattered all predictions by winning the primary by the razor-thin margin of 207,935 to 202,557. The election was decided on the industrial lakeshore, where Joe won all of the counties from Sheboygan to Kenosha. Any one of a number of factors by itself could have accounted for the upset: an election-eve drive by veterans to distribute McCarthy campaign literature all over the state, the decision by the influential Milwaukee *Journal* to remain neutral in the race, the hundreds of thousands of "personalized" postcards, Harold Townsend's zealous work in Milwaukee, McMurray's attacks, organized labor's unwillingness to back La Follette, Joe's feverish activity, La Follette's own half-hearted effort. At any rate, the election returns shocked political observers throughout the state and nation. Thomas Coleman told friends for years that news of La Follette's defeat was the happiest moment in his life.

McCarthy's primary victory virtually assured his election in November, but Democrat McMurray and his allies were far from willing to concede. They attempted to blacken McCarthy's record on the bench by charging that a judge could not legally run for the Senate (the State Supreme Court ruled otherwise), and they claimed falsely that McCarthy had ties with an ultraconservative "subversive" organization. In return, Joe called McMurray "Communistically inclined" and attempted to link him with the Communist *Daily Worker* and Reds within the C.I.O. This was a standard Republican tactic at the time and was in no way original with McCarthy. During one public debate Joe cleverly compared his own background with McMurray's by saying, "I'm just a farm boy, not a professor." The entire contest involved little more on both sides than name-calling and sloganeering.

The final tally matched McCarthy's private prediction almost exactly: he received 630,430 votes to McMurray's 378,772. He took seventy of the state's seventy-one counties and carried Milwaukee by a sizable margin. While he was not the leading G.O.P. vote-getter in the state, his victory was unquestionably impressive, even in that year of Republican landslides. One reporter predicted that the Senator-elect would be "a liberal Republican." When asked about his future plans, Joe simply returned to a familiar theme: "I don't claim to be any smarter than the next fellow, but I do claim that I work twice as hard and that's what I intend to do in Washington the next six years."

The first three years of McCarthy's life in Washington were relatively quiet and uneventful. Joe labored intensely on a number of projects, but his efforts yielded little legislation and a minimum of publicity. On Capitol Hill he was viewed as a very personable, somewhat conservative, at times unpredictable legislator who was distinguished in no special way. Only a few colleagues saw clearly in him the curious, anomalous characteristics of mind and emotion that would soon make him one of the most feared and despised men in the nation.

Joe's first notable involvement with legislation occurred in early 1947 when he became a passionate advocate of the decontrol of sugar, still being rationed under wartime authority by the federal government. He was responding to pleas by Wisconsin industries and housewives, and his efforts helped to accelerate decontrol. (Later attempts by political enemies to suggest collusion between McCarthy and sugar lobbyists do not withstand careful scrutiny.) In the course of his activities, however, he violated Senate traditions by harshly attacking a number of colleagues. He also displayed a penchant for unusual hyperbole. He called one Senator's amendment "completely meaningless," "completely deceptive," "fictitious," "ambiguous," "a mere well-meaning, pious hope and desire." During the same debate he falsely claimed to have just received information from the Department of Agriculture on world sugar supplies. When his bluff was called by a colleague who had telephoned Agriculture Secretary Clinton P. Anderson, McCarthy fired back, "Then, Mr. President, let me say that in view of the unquestioned figures, I do not give a tinker's damn what Secretary Anderson says about the matter." He proceeded to claim that Senator Ralph Flanders, an opponent on this issue, had told him earlier that he was going "to introduce some type of fictitious amendment which in effect will do nothing more nor less than deceive the housewife." That incorrect contention left Flanders sputtering in rage.

McCarthy also took a strong interest in the postwar housing issue and co-sponsored legislation creating a joint committee to study the matter. He angered a Senate colleague by finding a way to name a rather weak congressman chairman. He then accepted the vice-chairmanship for himself and proceeded to dominate the committee and a subcommittee for the next several months. Joe had a sincere desire to provide low-cost housing for disabled veterans; the health of the housing industry, the complexities of municipal codes, and the touchy question of public housing also concerned him. He was even more intent on using the housing issue to obtain publicity for himself. He especially desired to affix his name to an important piece of legislation.

McCarthy became something of an expert in housing, and he held scores of meetings and hearings on the overall issue throughout the country in late 1947 and early 1948. At times he got into nasty quarrels with witnesses and displayed a near total disregard for established committee procedure and even common courtesy. One conservative newspaper commented that the young senator "seems to aspire to the title of the Republican Huey Long." On the whole, however, his conduct was reasonably dignified and his actions productive.

After months of squabbling, the Eightieth Congress passed the Housing Bill of 1948, legislation McCarthy played a key role in creating. President Truman signed the bill but called it "emasculated," "fake," and "phony." He labelled all G.O.P. Congressmen callous "messenger boys" for the real estate lobby. (The charge would later be directed specifically at McCarthy, but with unconvincing evidence.) The positive features of the bill were largely ignored during the remainder of the election year and McCarthy received almost no credit for his many months of hard work. The following year he supported a liberal housing bill backed by the President, but his vote received little attention.

In 1949 McCarthy became emotionally involved in a Congressional investigation of the treatment of German SS troops convicted of massacring hundreds of disarmed American prisoners of war during the Battle of the Bulge. Despite much evidence to the contrary, the senator was absolutely convinced that Americans had abused the Germans and forced confessions out of them. The Malmedy case was virtually ignored in Wisconsin. No one in the Badger State, of German ancestry or otherwise, was concerned about the rights of convicted Nazi murderers. Those who did follow the affair were unlikely to become McCarthy supporters. Joe's capacity for un-swerving belief in a cause he considered righteous defied all reasonable evidence and argumentation to the contrary. His extreme hyperbole, his willingness to distort evidence, and his sometimes appalling lack of fairness and courtesy toward com-mittee witnesses had never been so vivid. Several Senate colleagues were again puzzled and offended by McCarthy's peculiar behavior toward his colleagues: in private he was always friendly and smiling; in public he could suddenly become vicious and abusive. Certainly the Malmedy hearings did nothing to enhance McCarthy's reputation, either in Washington or in Wisconsin.

Almost nothing Joe McCarthy did on Capitol Hill prior to 1950 attracted much favorable attention. And there was little likelihood that the situation would improve before he was up for relection in 1952. With the Democrats in control of Congress after the 1948 elections, Senator Burnet R. Maybank of South Carolina had McCarthy "bumped" from the Senate Banking and Currency Committee, saying that he would not sit beside the Wisconsin "troublemaker." Joe found himself shunted to the Committee on the District of Columbia, the least prestigious of all Senate committees. With that and a seat on the Expenditures in the Executive Departments Committee, Joe's opportunities for attracting public attention seemed extremely limited.

It was obvious to McCarthy that somehow in the near future he would have to find a way to construct a record he could stand on in 1952. This need was intensified by the fact that throughout 1949 he was under almost constant attack in Wisconsin by political opponents who attempted, among other things, to have him disbarred for being a Senate candidate three years earlier while continuing to serve as a circuit judge (a violation of the canons of judicial ethics of the American Bar Association). Joe sought advice from friends. He experimented with a variety of approaches. He was still not entirely certain what precise avenue to follow toward fame and reelection when he received an invitation from G.O.P. officials to make a Lincoln Day speaking tour. The first stop, on February 9, 1950, was scheduled for Wheeling, West Virginia.

Chapter 2 THE DISCOVERY OF ANTICOMMUNISM

RICHARD M. FRIED (b. 1941) is professor
of history at the University of Illinois-
Chicago. His book *Men Against McCarthy*
was based on his doctoral dissertation at
Columbia University. In this excerpt Fried
depicts McCarthy's earliest encounters with
the Reds-in-government issue. How did the
Wisconsin Senator get away with his initial
charges? Why was he taken seriously?

By 1950, McCarthy had demonstrated a talent for obstreperous disruption, but
no political benefits had accrued. Indeed, his abrasive behavior had closed a
number of doors to him. Thus, in 1949 he lost his seat on the Banking and
Currency Committee, partly because of GOP election losses but more directly
because Senator Burnet R. Maybank told Majority Leader Scott Lucas "that if
he wanted me to be chairman (of the committee) not to put McCarthy on it."
McCarthy was also losing ground back in Wisconsin. Alarming reports of his
past activities were circulating throughout the state; the Madison *Capital-Times*
was publishing accounts of the irregularities of his past campaigns and private
finances. Miles McMillin of the same paper had instituted a law suit on the
question of whether McCarthy had violated state law or bar association ethics
with his 1946 candidacy. Politicians have survived worse scandals, but not

Reprinted by permission from Richard M. Fried, *Men Against McCarthy* (New York: Columbia
University Press, 1976), pp. 40-52. Footnotes omitted.

without some compensatory stock in trade by which to reward the patience of their constituents. As of January 1950, the young Senator had no such political property.

The quest for a potent issue reportedly led McCarthy to a significant meeting on January 7, when he dined with Father Edmund A. Walsh, director of the School of Foreign Service at Georgetown University; Professor Charles H. Kraus, who taught political science at Georgetown and worked for McCarthy; and William A. Roberts, a Washington attorney. The three wished to make a more conscientious legislator of McCarthy. On his part, the Senator vented his anxiety over his failure to find an attractive political issue. Roberts suggested that he fight for the St. Lawrence Seaway. McCarthy, unimpressed, countered by asking his companions' views on the feasibility of pushing a modernized version of the Townsend Plan; they thought little of it. Father Walsh then remarked how salient the issue of communism had become. McCarthy, delighted with the idea, began to ponder its possibilities. The three men all tried to impress him with the need for a cautious, informed approach, but McCarthy, even this early did not heed the counsels of restraint; ultimately, when he proved to be a sorcerer's apprentice, all three were forced to disavow him.

Roy Cohn, McCarthy's aide at a later date, has offered the Senator's own purported version of his seizure of the communist issue. In November 1949, three patriots fretting at the inroads of communist subversion went to see McCarthy. Disturbed that an FBI report on this problem, to which they had access, had lain dormant in Pentagon files for two years, they had taken their data to three Republican Senators; but each resisted their entreaties for an offensive against communism. McCarthy carried their material home, became engrossed as he read it overnight, and called one of his mysterious informants at 6:30 A.M. to report that he was "buying the package"—much, says Cohn, as one would buy a used car. McCarthy's authorship of the tale weights the odds against its reliability, and his own testimony is contradictory. Asked in April 1950, how long ago he had discovered communism, he answered: "Two and a half months."

However, there is evidence that McCarthy had moved tentatively toward the communist issue before the celebrated "Dinner at the Colony." The historian Michael J. O'Brien has discovered a remarkable buried instance of McCarthy's use of the topic in November 1949, against political enemies in Wisconsin. In a speech in Madison on November 11 and in a memorandum which he sent to local opinion leaders heralding the talk, McCarthy insinuated that the Madison *Capital-Times*, published by his arch-foe William T. Evjue, was "the red mouthpiece for the Communist Party in Wisconsin." He founded this indictment chiefly on the claim that the city editor of the newspaper, Cedric Parker, was a Communist. McCarthy's enemies were vulnerable: Evjue himself had once called his employee a Communist; Parker was widely assumed to have been, if not a Communist, a fellow-traveler. McCarthy's documentation (much of it from

HUAC reports) was incomplete, but it sufficed to garner considerable newspaper coverage. *Time* magazine even picked up the story. As O'Brien has pointed out, the Cedric Parker affair taught McCarthy a lesson in the political utility of the communist issue.

However, even prior to his November 1949 assault on the *Capital-Times*, McCarthy had dabbled in anticommunism. He had made references to his "communistically inclined" opponent in 1946 and in a radio speech had asserted that much of the current "industrial unrest" could be "laid right smack at the door of the communists in the labor movement"; but these had been sporadic kidney punches, not a sustained barrage. In 1947, in his depredations upon public housing, he had labeled one housing project in New York a "breeding ground for Communism." In September 1949, urging the enactment of import quotas upon foreign furs, McCarthy managed to link the most parochial political concern to the campaign against communism. Not only did fur imports undermine American businesses, but since the bulk of the furs came from communist countries, each alien pelt earned dollars which subsidized Soviet spying in the United States.

At other times as well McCarthy, albeit fleetingly, raised the specter of communism. He inserted into the *Congressional Record* of October 19, 1949, material questioning the loyalty of some State Department officials. In arguing against the dismantling of German industrial plants, he suggested that some State Department personnel might be "more sympathetic to certain foreign ideologies than to our own." He went on to quote a news article critical of John Stewart Service, who allegedly had sold out the regime of Chiang Kai-shek. A few moments later, he called attention to an article assailing the State Department's "Two-Faced" foreign policy: while spending billions to halt communism in Europe, it was "playing the Soviet game in the Far East." In Kenosha on November 15, he again adverted to communist penetration of the State Department and to John Stewart Service. He scorned America's benighted foreign policy once more in a December 3 speech in Philadelphia; two days later in Milwaukee, he blamed the State Department for the "tremendous pace" at which the nation was losing ground in the cold war. To a Madison audience he explained that he had voted against the reappointment of Leland Olds to the Federal Power Commission "because he is a Communist." On January 5, 1950, McCarthy mounted another attack on Service and those who had espoused the cause of the Chinese Reds.

The Hiss case greatly impressed McCarthy. Its outcome made it urgent, said McCarthy, that Acheson "either clean the Communists out of the State Department or resign and let President Truman appoint someone who will." On January 25, the Wisconsinite interrupted Senator Karl Mundt's declamation on the meaning of the Hiss case to ask if Mundt had heard Acheson's "fantastic statement" made moments before, when he announced his refusal to turn his back on Hiss. Was the Secretary implying that "he will not turn his back on any other Communists in the State Department...?" Two weeks later, McCarthy again broached the issue of communist infiltration. He read a news article asserting that one of the top communist spies in government—unnamed—was using a Justice of the Supreme Court—also unnamed—as a "front." Since the matter fell outside the jurisdiction of his own committee, McCarthy marked it for the attention of the appropriate panel. Clearly, the issue of communism was percolating through McCarthy's mind well before the Wheeling speech and, indeed, the Colony dinner.

It would be wrong, however, to exaggerate either McCarthy's interest or preparation in anticommunism prior to his Lincoln Day offensive. In the early weeks of 1950, he was searching for an issue that would increase his visibility. He even toyed with Senator Estes Kefauver's eventual concern, the growth of crime, suggesting that the Senate investigate "whether racketeers and gamblers...are attempting to control city politics." He continued to dally with the question of old age pensions. Advance publicity for his Wheeling speech mentioned not a word about his credentials, fresh as they were, as an anticommunist. While he had not announced the subject of his address, the Wisconsin Senator, according to the Wheeling *News-Register*, would probably discuss "the controversial Brannan plan, aid to disabled and aged, and other timely topics." The Wheeling *Intelligencer* touted him as "one of Washington's most ardent champions of adequate old age and other pensions and it is quite sure that he will voice his sentiments along these lines" on February 9.

For his speech, McCarthy had hastily assembled a collage of snippets from the utterances of several more established spokesmen for Republican anti-communism. On arrival, he gave out copies of a "rough draft" of the speech to the press and radio, but then went to his hotel room to work on the text until shortly before the banquet. For the Ohio County Women's Republican Club, McCarthy sketched the harsh, steely outlines of the cold war and the unbridgeable differences in morality and ideology dividing Russia, with its "communist atheism," from the Christian West. And now, the Senator warned, "the chips are down—they are truly down." In 1945, the free world contained 1,625,000,000 souls while communism claimed only 180,000,000. Now the odds had shifted: 800,000,000 people lay under communist subjugation (and others had gone neutralist) while the free world numbered 500,000,000 people. America had lost ground not as a result of foreign aggression, but "because of the traitorous actions of those who have been treated so well by this nation," who enjoyed "the finest homes, the finest college education, and the finest jobs in Government we can give." This was "glaringly true in the State Department," where "the bright young men who are born with silver spoons in their mouths are the ones who have been worst." McCarthy named John Stewart Service, Mary Jane Keeney, Gustavo Duran, and Harlow Shapley as examples. Tantalizingly, he intimated

> While I cannot take the time to name all of the men in the State Department who have been named as members of the Communist Party and members of a spy ring, I have here in my hand a list of 205. . . a list of names that were made known to the Secretary of State and who nevertheless are still working and shaping the policy of the State Department.

Or so his opponents claimed he said. McCarthy himself later maintained that he had used the number "fifty-seven" Communists or party loyalists. Neither McCarthy nor his critics were able to document their assertions conclusively. . . .

From the welter of conflicting (and not always disinterested) testimony, no fully satisfactory account of the speech has emerged. Only possibilities remain. McCarthy may have said 205, or he may have corrected this to 57 as he did in subsequent addresses. He might even have used both figures—either in confusion and inadvertence or perhaps, as he himself conjectured, with 57 as the key number and 205 in a lesser role. In any case, he had no list at all; the figure 205 was a deduction from a four-year-old letter from then-Secretary of State James F. Byrnes to Congressman Adolph Sabath regarding the screening of some 4,000 prospective employees transferred to State from wartime agencies. Byrnes reported that recommendations against further employment had been made in the cases of 285 of these individuals, of whom 79 had been "separated from service."

McCarthy added to the muddle by several alterations of his text in the course of his journey. When his plane put down in Milwaukee, he dodged reporters, but during a stop-over in Denver on February 10 he submitted to an interview. He claimed he had a list of 207 State Department employees whom he now labeled "bad risks"; at the same time, he elaborated, he knew of 57 "card-carrying" Communists in the department. He even offered to display the list—no, wait, it was in his luggage on the plane. In a radio interview the same day in Salt Lake City, McCarthy declared that in Wheeling he had exposed the retention of 57 "card-carrying" Communists in Foggy Bottom. If the Secretary of State wanted their names, he had only to call—but Acheson should first "show his sincerity" by rolling back the President's 1948 order which had rendered the employee loyalty files confidential. On February 11, from Reno, McCarthy dispatched a telegram to the President trumpeting the presence of 57 Communists in the State Department. He challenged Truman to ask Acheson why of the "approximately 300" (i.e., the 285 of the Byrnes letter) certified by the Department's Loyalty Review Board for discharge only about 80 had been dismissed, and then only "after lengthy consultation with Alger Hiss."

As the publicity increased, the hedges McCarthy placed about his original utterances sprouted profusely. To a reporter in Reno, he denied having called "traitors" the four persons he had named. "And you will notice I didn't call them Communists either." He conceded that he "should have had a line in there saying they were specific cases of people with Communistic connections." He had also crossed out the number 205 from his manuscript and substituted 57. Even so, his warning to a Reno Republican gathering about "57 card-carrying members" of the Communist Party elicited gasps and, in some cases, tears from his audience. Then he was off to Las Vegas for another speech on February 13; the next day, at a press conference in Los Angeles, McCarthy restated the conditions on which he would yield his 57 names. He offered his message ("57 active Communists") to the Republican faithful of Huron, South Dakota, grabbed a quick nightcap, and went winging back to Washington by way of Milwaukee and Appleton, having left behind a trail of contradictory news accounts and the seeds of disputes which would rage for years.

One of the mysteries of the McCarthy era is, however, the manner in which these garbled declarations to chicken-and-peas party ceremonial convocations shortly became the stuff of which history is made. Amid the Lincoln Day oratory of such formidable GOP spokesmen as Richard Nixon, Kenneth Wherry, John Bricker, and Guy Gabrielson, news reports of the Wheeling speech were few. While the wire-service dispatches from Wheeling may have alerted reporters to hunt up McCarthy at the Milwaukee and Denver airports, it was his personal challenge to Truman and the official response to his utterances which made his charges newsworthy: the first articles in the *New York Times* and Washington *Post* headlined McCarthy's telegram to the President and carried the State Department's denial of his claims.

Hitting upon the communist issue as it reached full ripeness, McCarthy benefited from good timing. The fall of China, Russia's A-bomb, Hiss, Fuchs, the H-bomb decision—these events could not help but register upon the public consciousness. Equally important, other Republicans had begun in earnest to box the compass of espionage revelations and the administration's laxity in regard to security. Thus, Senator Homer Capehart asserted on February 4 that there were other spies besides Fuchs, "and there will continue to be as long as we have a President who refers to such matters as 'red herrings' and a Secretary of State who refuses to turn his back on the Alger Hisses." On February 14, Karl Mundt charged that for eighteen years the nation had been "run by New Dealers, Fair Dealers, Misdealers and Hiss dealers who have shuttled back and forth between Freedom and Red Fascism like a pendulum on a kukoo clock." The GOP's statement of principles, released on February 6, showed the party's intention to make a major campaign issue of the loyalty program and communist subversion; many Lincoln Day speeches gave testimony of that inclination.

Yet why was it the novice McCarthy who emerged as the leading exponent of anticommunism? Since his potshots were part of a general Republican salvo, the State Department may have accorded him undue prominence simply by singling out his charges. While the numerical specificity of McCarthy's claims made them unusually vulnerable, the State Department's denials seemed only to give the charges greater newsworthiness. The administration's jumpiness in regard to the loyalty-security question may have prompted what one journalist called its "quick reaction." Arthur Krock reported that the Democrats knew the topic had "explosive and destructive potentials" and that Truman, while wanly hopeful that the issue would not damage his party badly in the next election, was scrupulously avoiding any further "red herring" remarks.

For whatever reason, the State Department made McCarthy its target. On February 10, press officer Lincoln White scouted the Wheeling assertions: the Department had identified no Communists in its employ, "and if we find any they will be summarily discharged." The next day, Deputy Undersecretary of State John Puerifoy wired McCarthy to ask for the 205 names. On February 13, Puerifoy told reporters he knew of no Reds in his department. "But if I can find a single one," he assured them, "I will have him fired before sundown." At his February 16 press conference, President Truman exclaimed that there "was not a word of truth in what the Senator said." Scott M. Lucas, the Democratic Majority Leader, stated that if he had made McCarthy's statements, "I would be ashamed of myself for the rest of my life."

Although these remarks by administration spokesman constituted something of a challenge, McCarthy himself apparently took the initiative which led to the Senate confrontation of February 20 over his charges. . . .

Obtaining the floor late in the day on February 20, McCarthy outlined his charges and strove to tidy up the figures which had been quoted in the past ten days. He explained that he had extrapolated the number 205 from Byrnes's 1946 letter; it was the difference—or nearly so—between 285, the number of security risks or undesirables of whom Byrnes had been apprised by a personnel screening board, and 79, the number of these who had been discharged shortly after. Amid much badgering, mostly by Senator Lucas, McCarthy repeated what purported to be his Wheeling speech. The text he read spoke of "57 cases of individuals who would appear to be either card-carrying members or certainly loyal to the Communist Party." His radioactive 57 had a short half-life; no longer would he even certify that they were all card-carrying Communists. McCarthy also noted that the Wheeling and Reno speeches had been recorded, "so there is no question about what I said. I do not believe I mentioned the figure 205. I believe I said 'over 200.'" Some, but not all, of the 57 were among these 205. Lucas gratingly insisted upon the exact language used in Wheeling, noting newspaper references to 205 Communists, but McCarthy stood fast.

McCarthy moved on to a recital of information taken, he said, from the files of 81 State Department employees of questionable loyalty—thus a new figure entered the calculations. It later developed that McCarthy had derived this data from a collection of summaries of 108 loyalty files culled out in 1947 by the staff of the House Appropriations Committee as a sampling of the effectiveness of the State Department loyalty program. First examined by a subcommittee of the

House Appropriations Committee, the "108 list" received scrutiny from three other committees and provided ammunition for several speeches. Perhaps fifteen or twenty Congressmen knew of the list when McCarthy came back from his Wheeling junket; he may have acquired the dossiers from one of them or from a committee staff member. On February 20, McCarthy had no names—only a batch of excerpts labeled anonymously by number. Of the 108 individuals (some of them mere applicants for employment in the first place), only 57 remained in the State Department at the time the 108 list was drawn up—hence McCarthy's "57 Communists."

As McCarthy labored through his cases, the few Democrats on the floor continued to snipe at him. Why, queried Herbert H. Lehman, had he not immediately submitted his 57 names to the State Department? Lucas demanded the name of case number 1; McCarthy replied that he preferred to reveal the names in executive session before the appropriate committee, but, if the Senate so desired, he would release the names. When McCarthy reached case number 14, Senator Wherry, the Republican floor leader, suggested the absence of a quorum. (Ten or so were present.) This fact confirmed, Lucas made the unusual demand that the sergeant-at-arms request the presence of the absent Senators. Lucas then moved adjournment, but his parliamentary ploy was defeated, eighteen to sixteen. All eighteen negative votes were cast by Republicans; all sixteen affirmative, by Democrats. A quorum was obtained, and McCarthy continued. Thereupon Senator Brien McMahon, who had hurried back to the floor in evening dress, began to grill McCarthy on whether he was reading only the derogatory information in the files. McCarthy so stipulated, but he questioned the relevance of data on whether a suspect was "good to his wife and children and all that sort of thing." McMahon countered that McCarthy's method, precluding a balanced assessment of the data, smacked of the "star chamber." McCarthy retorted that by this criterion Lucas, who had insisted he name names, was the worst offender.

When McCarthy finally concluded his eighty-one cases, they fell far short of proving Communist infiltration of the State Department. One case, by his own admission, dealt not with a subversive at all, but with a loyal American who did not get a job. Another raised no question "insofar as communistic activities are concerned," but suggested "rather unusual mental aberrations" of which delicacy prevented disclosure. Similarly, case number 77 repeated case number 9, cases 3 and 4 were the same, and four cases got lost in the shuffle. Only later did it become clear that these dossiers were simply warmed-over remains, sampled and forgotten by others.

Despite the evident puncturability of McCarthy's arguments, the Democrats did not riposte effectively. Senator Lucas, leader of the corporal's guard of Democrats present for the entire speech, was primed to the extent that he had clippings of McCarthy's speeches in front of him. As he persisted in interrupting

McCarthy, however, he gave the impression of having lost sight of the distinction between rebuttal and harassment. His thrusts lacked finesse. He tried to pin McCarthy down on his "numbers game," but pending evidence obtained from Wheeling (in itself inconclusive), McCarthy's explanation was at least plausible. Moreover, it is unlikely that the proof of inconsistencies in the use of numbers and labels convinced many onlookers, except those already hostile to McCarthy, that he was perpetrating a sham. Similarly, Lucas did not occupy the firmest ground in daring McCarthy to name names. Much subsequent criticism of the Senator from Wisconsin focused on occasions when he did name names. Interjections by other Democrats also failed generally to hit the mark.

Yet if tactics of rebuttal brought few returns, a strategy of silence was little likelier to succeed, for the Republicans were already too aware of the utility of the communist issue. The proceedings of February 20 made clear that McCarthy could count on support from his party. Fellow Republicans aided him with friendly leading questions, ran parliamentary interference, and applauded his efforts. Homer Ferguson, who had apparently brought in his own files on the eighty-one cases, assisted his young colleague through their complexities and did nothing to destroy the fiction that McCarthy was presenting new and arcane data smuggled out of the remotest warrens of Foggy Bottom.

Chapter 3   TO BE CALLED BEFORE THE McCARTHY COMMITTEE

JAMES A. WECHSLER (1915-1983) was an editorial-page editor and columnist for the liberal *New York Post*. As a student at Columbia University he joined the Young Communist League (YCL), resigning in 1937 at the age of twenty-two. During the early 1950s Wechsler and the *Post* were frequently critical of McCarthy, and in 1953 the journalist found himself seated in front of the McCarthy committee listening to menacing reminders of his youthful rendezvous with Reds. Is there sufficient evidence in this selection to conclude that McCarthy was a demagogue?

The hearing had been scheduled to begin at 3 o'clock, but it did not actually get under way until seventy minutes later. I spent the interval pacing the corridor of the Senate Office Building with Shannon and wondering whether the delay was a stratagem designed to try the nerves of the witness. That suspicion proved unfounded: the delay was a result of Wayne Morse's refusal to permit unanimous consent for a committee hearing while the Senate was in session.

This was an executive session, and the press and public were barred. When I walked into the spacious hearing room McCarthy was seated at the head of the table. At his side was Roy Cohn looking like a precocious college sophomore visiting Washington during spring recess. Nearby was [Hearst reporter Howard] Rushmore, slouched uncomfortably in a chair that, like most chairs, was too small to hold him. My seat was at the opposite end of the table, facing McCarthy. On my

From *The Age of Suspicion* by James A. Wechsler. Copyright 1953 by James A. Wechsler. Reprinted by permission of Random House, Inc. Pp. 266-288. Footnotes omitted.

left, a few feet back, as if keeping at a respectful distance from McCarthy, were G. David Schine and Don Surine, neither of whom uttered a word throughout the proceedings. On my right was the only conceivably friendly face in the room—Senator Henry Jackson, a former Representative just elected to the Senate from the State of Washington.

When I entered McCarthy stood up stiffly and motioned me to the witness chair. Disarmingly, he asked me how I pronounced my last name. I was tempted to respond that he had pronounced it correctly on television but I resolved to fight such temptation. I answered the question.

Then McCarthy began in his low, unprovocative voice: "Mr. Wechsler, we are sorry we kept you waiting but there originally was an objection to this committee sitting this afternoon by Senator Morse, and we had to wait for permission to sit."

I replied that I understood.

"I may say," he continued, speaking quite swiftly and softly so that I almost had difficulty hearing him, "the reason for your being called today is that you are one of the many authors of books whose books have been used in the Information Program in various libraries, and we would like to check into a number of matters. Mr. Cohn will do the questioning."

Cohn took over briefly for a review of the names and dates of my published works. He elicited the fact that two of the books—*Revolt on the Campus* and *War Our Heritage*—were written when I was a member of the YCL. Then he jumped quickly to nonliterary fields and, during most of the remainder of the two hearings, little attention was devoted to the ostensible subject of the hearings—the books I had written. First he established that I had used the name "Arthur Lawson" on my YCL membership card.

"Let me add," I said, "that it was a name I was given when I joined and that I never used it again."

Cohn dropped the subject. Now he wanted to know how long I had been a member of the YCL. I gave him the answer and added that the whole chronology had already been published in the *Congressional Record* in the statement that Senator Lehman had inserted at my request.

The committee's researchers were apparently unaware of the existence of the document and wanted to know the date.

McCarthy seemed only mildly interested in Cohn's questioning; he was getting ready to take over himself. After another moment, he jumped in.

"May I interrupt, Mr. Cohn?" McCarthy asked and, without waiting for an answer, he interrupted at length, while Cohn maintained a sulky silence, like a star pupil whom teacher has pushed aside.

"Mr. Wechsler, do you have any other people who are members of the Young Communist League, who were or are members of the Young Communist League, working for you on your newspaper?"

The fight was beginning rather sooner than I had expected, and on ground I had hardly expected him to invade so casually.

This was the first of many questions that I answered fully despite my belief that they were far beyond the scope of the committee's authorized inquiry. I had resolved much earlier that silence was suicidal in dealing with McCarthy. I know some thoughtful people differ with me, and that there are some who believe I should have refused to answer any questions dealing with the policies and personnel of the newspaper I edit. But I was persuaded then, and I have not changed my opinion, that McCarthy was hoping I would refuse to testify so that he could use my silence to charge that I had something to hide. I was not trying to "convince" McCarthy of anything; I was trying to write a record that could be read intelligibly by bemused Americans who might still believe that McCarthy was interested in truth. To put it simply, I did not believe that my answers would tend to incriminate or degrade me but I was quite certain that silence would.

"I will say that I am going to answer that question because I believe it is a citizen's responsibility to testify. before a Senate committee whether he likes the committee or not," I said.

"I know you do not like this committee," McCarthy interjected tonelessly, as if to assure me at once that he was impervious to personal offense and as if he had forgotten that he had repeatedly refused to testify before a Senate committee because he considered it hostile to him.

"I want to say that I think you are now exploring a subject which the American Society of Newspaper Editors might want to consider at some length," I continued.

"I answer the question solely because I recognize your capacity for misinterpretation of a failure to answer. I answer it with the protest signified. To my knowledge there are no communists on the staff of the New York *Post* at this time."

What about former communists, McCarthy wanted to know. I identified them. There were four, and in each case they were men whose past affiliations were as well known as their present anti-communism.

Thus, in less than five minutes, an investigation allegedly directed at my work as an author of books in use by United States Information Service libraries had become an examination of the staff of the *Post*. There had been no indication as to what books of mine were found overseas, or any discussion of their content.

Now McCarthy got to his real point:

"You see your books, some of them, were paid for by taxpayers' money. They are being used, allegedly, to fight communism. Your record, as far as I can see it, has not been to fight communism. You have fought every man who has ever tried to fight communism, as far as I know. Your paper, in my opinion, is next to and almost paralleling the *Daily Worker*. We are curious to know, therefore, why your books were purchased. We want to know how many communists, if any, you still have working for you."

This was quite a speech; it was a summary of everything that he had to say in that hearing and the one that followed. Listening to it I had to resist the competing emotions of anger and hopelessness. But I had brought with me a document that I naively considered a devastating rebuttal. Since McCarthy had delivered what almost sounded like his summation before the hearing had barely begun, I decided to use it at once.

So I asked permission to insert in the record of the hearing the statement issued on December 28, 1952, by the National Committee of the Communist Party reviewing the previous election and especially the failure of the Progressive Party ticket to roll up a meaningful vote: it had in fact obtained only a small fraction of the disappointing Wallace vote of 1948. In the course of this analysis the communist chieftains declared:

> Support of the pro-war measures of the Truman administration; acceptance and propagation of the "Big Lie" of the external and internal "communist menace" disarmed the workers, blocked the path to independent political action by labor and its allies and paved the way for a Republican victory.
>
> The major responsibility for this policy and its consequences rests squarely with the reformist and Social Democratic trade-union officialdom. This was the content of the policies of the Reuthers, Dubinskys, Wechslers et al who paralyzed independent political action by projecting the myth that Stevenson was an obstacle to the advance of reaction. They pursued these policies despite the fact that the Democratic Party administration, operating with bipartisan support, originated and unfolded the current war program in behalf of Wall Street.

This communist jargon was simply a way of affirming what I had long believed—that the most effective opponents of communism in America have been the liberals and labor leaders associated with the non-communist Left. Offering the document as an exhibit, I said: "I am rather fond of this tribute, and it may perhaps have some bearing on your comment that I have not been active in fighting communism."

In a cold, casual voice McCarthy responded quickly:

"Did you have anything to do with the passage of that resolution? Did you take any part in promoting the passage of that resolution?"

I thought I had expected anything, but my imagination had been inadequate. His words registered slowly. I must have looked baffled as well as astonished, almost incapable of trusting my own senses.

"Is that a serious question?" I asked.

McCarthy turned briskly to the stenographer.

"Will you read the question to the witness?"

His voice was harder and tougher. In this strange proceeding he alternately played the role of prosecutor and judge, and now he was definitely the prosecutor. The stenographer read the question.

I knew I was making an obvious effort to keep my voice down as I answered, and I am sure my hands trembled a little:

"Sir, I have not been in any way affiliated with the communist movement since late 1937, as I believe your investigation will show. That resolution was adopted by the Communist Party as a tribute to the militant and vigorous anti-communism of the New York *Post* which has, in my judgment, been more effective in leading people away from communism, Senator, than those who prefer to identify liberalism with communism."

He let me finish and then, in the same flat tone, he said:

"Now will you answer the question?"

"The answer is no, Senator," I replied.

"The answer is no. Do you know whether anyone on your staff took part in promoting the passage of that resolution?"

"Senator, to the best of my knowledge, no one on my staff is a member of the Central Committee of the Communist Party or identified with it in any way."

"Now will you answer the question? Will you read the question to the witness?"

"I have answered it as best I can."

"You have said that you did not think anyone on your staff was a part of the committee. That was not the question. Read the question to the witness."

The stenographer read it. The faint smile which McCarthy had exhibited earlier was gone now. Once again, in a voice that must have sounded quite spiritless, I answered the question.

"I do not know that anyone on my staff took any part in promoting the passage of that resolution," I said. He had astounded me, and he knew it.

Thus, within ten minutes after the hearing had begun, I found myself in the preposterous position of denying under oath that I had inspired the long series of communist attacks against me, climaxed by the denunciation of the Central Committee.

With that single stroke of what Philip Graham, publisher of the Washington *Post,* later described as "brute brilliance," McCarthy thus virtually ruled out the whole structure of evidence which I had wide-eyedly assumed would resolve the issue once and for all. Here indeed was a daring new concept in which the existence of evidence of innocence becomes the damning proof of guilt. This is the way it must feel to be committed to a madhouse through some medical mistake; everything is turned upside down. What had heretofore constituted elementary reasonableness is viewed by everyone else as a quaint eccentricity; the most absurd remark becomes the commonplace.

McCarthy reverted to the same thesis several times. Each time he did so with total blandness, as though only the dullest or most subversive mind could detect anything extraordinary in his approach.

He had at last spelled out the formula under which our whole society could be transformed into a universe of suspicion. What a man had said or done could no longer be accepted as bearing the slightest relationship to what he was or what he believed. More likely, it was a disguise to conceal his hidden allegiances to exactly the reverse of what he claimed to stand for. At the second hearing he was to develop this theme even more spectacularly.

McCarthy went on to resume his study of *Post* staff members. Each one mentioned had a long record of anti-communist activity—longer, for example, than Rushmore's. Any books I had written which might have found their way into the overseas libraries were far away and forgotten. This had become an unconcealed investigation of a newspaper which had taken an uncharitable view of Joe McCarthy. When he had finished talking about personnel, he shifted at once to editorial policy.

"Have you been making attacks upon J. Edgar Hoover in the editorial columns of your paper?" he asked abruptly.

"Sir, the New York *Post* has on a couple of occasions carried editorials critical of the FBI. We do not regard any Government agency as above criticism. I assume your committee doesn't either. We have at the same time taken very strongly the position that the charge that the FBI is a Gestapo or a fascist agency was an unfounded, unwarranted charge."

McCarthy maintains a curiously ambivalent relationship to the FBI. Much of what he has done plainly implies that the Bureau is incapable of protecting the country from subversion; although a late starter, he has indicated in a variety of ways that the fight against communism did not really begin until he entered it. Yet he has simultaneously pictured himself as the FBI's truest defender. Actually, the editorials to which he called attention had dealt with the phenomenon of immunity from criticism achieved by the FBI. At the time of the attempt on Victor Reuther's life, the *Post* editorially lamented what we felt was the failure of the FBI to step into the case promptly; at the time of the escape of Gerhard Eisler and the flight of the seven convicted communist leaders, we had whimsically observed that poor Dean Acheson or some other Democratic bureaucrat would have been given a terrible beating in Congress if these events had occurred within their jurisdiction. J. Edgar Hoover has been the object of irresponsible abuse from the communists; that does not absolve him from criticism from other sources. It is certainly to his credit that the FBI has not run wild, as secret-police agencies in other countries have done, but the surest guarantee against excesses is the preservation of the public's right to examine the FBI at least as freely as the State Department. No one, to my knowledge, has advanced the contention that editorial writers should cease and desist from all criticism of a Secretary of State simply because—as in the case of both Acheson and Dulles—he is also being denounced by the Moscow radio.

Now McCarthy was asking:

"Have you always been very critical of the heads of the Un-American Activities Committee? You have always thought they were very bad men."

I confessed that I had never spoken highly of J. Parnell Thomas, who went from

Congress to jail. For the record, however, I presented a letter I had received early in 1950 from a man who had been one of the Republicans on that committee. It read:

Dear Mr. Wechsler:

This is just a note to tell you that I thought your editorial on the Hiss case, published in your issue of January 23rd, was one of the most able and fair appraisals of a very difficult problem which I have seen.

Since you probably have me categorized as one of the "reactionaries" mentioned in your editorial, I thought you might be particularly interested in my reaction.

With all good wishes,

Sincerely yours,
Richard Nixon.

"I would like to submit that," I said.

'You may put that in," McCarthy replied, betraying no more concern about this exhibit than earlier ones. "I would like to have you get back to my question, then, if you could, however."

I yielded.

"If it is a momentous issue, Senator," I said, "I am unable to present any documents suggesting that I praised a Chairman of the House Un-American Activities Committee."

McCarthy pressed the point.

"The principal villains in your book are those who have gone about the job of exposing communists. Is that correct? Or is that an unfair statement?"

"No, Senator, that is not correct. I may say, since you have asked the question, that we have repeatedly taken the position that the New York *Post* is as bitterly opposed to Joe Stalin as it is to Joe McCarthy, and we believe that a free society can combat both."

Now we were off.

Q. And you are opposed to Bill Jenner, too. You think he is a dangerous man?

A. Senator, I give you a priority in that field. I have not written about Senator Jenner in recent months. With respect to the activities of the Senator's committee, I have not criticized the work of its counsel, Mr. Robert Morris.

Q. Do you think Jenner is doing a good job?

A. Senator, I assume you do not want me to make speeches here, and I am trying not to. However, when you ask me a question like that, it is difficult not to respond with a speech.

Q. You can answer that in as great length as you care to. We have a lot of time.

A.   My basic position is that American society is a very strong and resilient one. I believe we have successfully resisted communist aggression in the world under the leadership of men whom you have at times deemed sinister. I believe that in the battle of ideas we can compete effectively with the communists any day of the week without resorting to methods which I regard as imitative of theirs. I see by your expression that you feel you have heard this before, so I will not pursue the point.

Q.   I have. I have read it in the *Daily Worker* and in the New York *Post*.

A.   You have probably read it in the New York *Times*. I can't help wonder when the editor of the *Times* is going to be down here.

Q.   Will you get back to that question after a while? The question is: do you think Bill Jenner is doing a good job?

A.   I am not an enthusiast of Senator Jenner's.

Cohn tried to get back into the dialogue but McCarthy brushed him aside and the young man slumped back, watching the master with what seemed to be a blend of reverence and resentment. Now McCarthy was shifting from point to point and back again so that no issue could be thoroughly disposed of before another had arisen; it was at this juncture that I realized I was beginning to watch him as though I were seated at the press table rather than in the witness chair, and that it was almost a physical effort to resume the role of participant.

Suddenly he had changed the scene. Had I known Harry Dexter White? I replied that I had met him once, for approximately two minutes, when I returned to Washington from Germany. I went to his office to obtain my formal release from the Treasury Department so that I could go back to journalism.

"Is there any doubt in your mind that Harry Dexter White was at that time a communist agent?" McCarthy asked, as if presenting the simplest question in the world.

"Senator, I haven't any personal knowledge of Harry Dexter White. If you are asking me my opinions based on hearsay and reading, that is quite a different matter. But I must confess that I hesitate to pronounce a certain answer about a dead man."

Then we got back to the *Post* staff, and there were the same insinuations and the same responses, and then back to the FBI for another attempt to prove I had been unco-operative about prosecuting communists. On McCarthy's premise my deficiency was clear; I had never described any intimacy with a single communist espionage agent, which was utterly true. Beside this great and devastating truth it seemed almost inconsequential for me to suggest that the explanation of my passivity was the drab fact that I had not known any spies.

Had I ever talked to the FBI? The answer was yes; whenever an FBI agent came to see me about someone I had known applying for a Government post, I gave as much information as I had; I always emphasized that I had no first-hand knowledge extending beyond 1937 and cautioned that others might have changed their views as decisively as I had.

I know there are some former communists who have conscientiously declined to give any information about others than themselves. I confronted that problem a long time ago and the answer I reached was that there was no justification for a vow of silence. The communist movement was not an amiable secret society to which one owed a personal loyalty after abandoning membership in it. There is abundant evidence that it it a tough, disciplined world-wide movement dedicated to the destruction of free society. I am willing to defend its right to conduct public propaganda functions because I believe there is ample margin of safety in our system and because I am convinced that communist ideas can best be met and overcome in open debate. But to defend that principle of open expression is not to argue that there is an obligation to protect communists seeking strategic positions in Government. Liberals who maintain this opinion would have been the first, I think, to rebuke a professed ex-Nazi who declined to identify his former associates in Government at a time when Nazism was sweeping over Europe.

McCarthy seemed impatient as I responded:

"Where I have been asked about people I knew at that time [of my communist membership], I answered freely and fully. If I knew today that someone who had been in the Young Communist League with me was in a strategic Government post, I would certainly communicate that information. There has never been any question in my mind as to a citizen's responsibility on that point, and I do not believe the FBI would suggest that I have been unco-operative in the discussion of such cases."

But had I ever given the FBI a full list of everyone I had known?

The answer was that no such dragnet question, I am glad to say, had ever been asked me by the FBI. In 1948 I had given Louis Nichols, now the Deputy Chief of the FBI, a detailed statement of my own past connections; I had done so because of an incident involving Nancy which revealed that the FBI file on us was seriously incomplete. She had been serving as counsel for the Truman Committee on Civil Rights when a question was abruptly raised about her past membership in the YCL—a point she had fully discussed with an FBI agent after she went to work for the Government. When I heard that had been raised again, I went to see Nichols and we talked it out and the matter was cleared up.

"Do you know any of those Young Communists who are in any Government position today?" McCarthy asked.

"No, I do not."

"Do you know Bernard De Voto?"

"I trust this is not a sequitur," I replied.

"Pardon?"

"I trust this is not a sequitur."

"It is a question."

"I believe I may have met Bernard De Voto. I can't recall the occasion on which I did. I regret to say that he is not a close personal friend of mine."

"You regret to say that?"

"Yes, sir."

"You did not collaborate with him in writing the article in which he advocated that Americans not talk to the FBI?"

"No, sir, I thought that was a very bad article."

"You do not agree with that?"

"I don't agree with that."

This exchange compressed into half a minute a whole range of McCarthy devices. First there was the sudden introduction of De Voto's name into a discussion dealing with the identity of former communists; he happens to be a distinguished American scholar who never roamed into communist territory. Then there was the intimation that De Voto's article on the FBI was proof he was a traitor and that I not only sanctioned the article but had helped him write it (presumably in that spare time when I was not writing communist denunciations of myself). It was almost a case of guilt by non-association.

Then McCarthy announced:

"We are going to ask you, Mr. Wechsler, to prepare a list and submit it to the committee and consider it to be submitted under oath, of all the Young Communist Leaguers that you knew as such, or the communists."

This was the final gambit. I had characterized myself as a "responsible but not friendly witness." From the start, whether rightly or wrongly, I had believed that what McCarthy was seeking was the chance to walk out of the hearing room and tell the press that I had "balked." Once he was able to do that, I would be engaged in the hopeless pursuit of headlines describing me as just another reluctant witness. And from that point on McCarthy would proceed to discredit the *Post* because I had refused to testify freely before a Senate committee.

There may be some splendor in such a role but on the whole it escapes me. By and large liberals have believed in giving wide scope to congressional committees. Moreover, there is in the American tradition a very real belief that the man who has nothing to conceal will speak up when spoken to; muteness has not often been equated with valor. Back in 1947, in an article in the *Guild Reporter,* I had written:

It would be nice if the world were prettier, but it isn't; espionage and sabotage are facts of modern life. I have no brief for anybody who refuses to testify before a congressional committee; no matter how foolish or fierce the committee, an American ought to be prepared to state his case in any public place at any time.

Believing this, I had gone along answering everything and now I faced what

McCarthy undoubtedly regarded as the great question. I am sure that he knew enough about me to guess the reluctance with which I would give such a list to a man like him. I am also confident that he would have felt he had finally cornered me if I now refused to give it to him. Then, and for many days after, it was a rather strange duel. For McCarthy knew I would have been happier not to give him any list and I knew he would have been delighted if I had taken that stand.

All this, let me add, was clearer to me after the hearing than at that moment. The demand for the list was an almost parenthetical remark; my answer was an oblique comment about the obvious absurdity of asking a man to remember everyone whom he had known in a different context nearly sixteen years before.

"I don't know that you would be able to do very well with a similar list of any organization that you were connected with sixteen years ago," I said.

"Well, we are asking for the list. You say you have severed your connection. I am not going to, at this time, try to—"

"Senator, you are raising that point," I interrupted.

He went on as if I were inaudible.

"—pass on whether that is true or not. I know that you never testified in a case against an ex-communist. I know that none of the men you have named here as anti-communists ever testified in a case against communists. I know that they and you have been consistently and viciously attacking anyone who does testify against communists, anyone that exposes communists—"

"Senator, that is not true."

"Let me finish. You may have all the time in the world to talk. So you cannot blame the average person who questions whether you ever did break with the party."

There it was again, and not for the last time; and each time he said it I had a feeling of rage tinged with futility. Senator Jackson was listening attentively, with manifest concern, and at various points along the way he helped me clarify the record; but how could one break through the ring of fantasy that McCarthy was constructing? If each exhibit of my anti-communism were merely additional evidence that I had led a truly gigantic political double life, what remained to be said that had any meaning?

Except for Jackson the room seemed full of the dull, smirking faces of McCarthy's staff watching their bully-boy in action and trying to show him that they were on his side and getting a big kick our of his performance. Occasionally I glanced at Rushmore, who never returned my gaze; he, of all people, knew the magnitude of the fraud and was perfectly willing to be an accomplice in it. Some years earlier we had both been active members of the anti-communist faction in the Newspaper Guild and he could not have forgotten that; as a Guild member he also knew all the details of the internal battle on *PM*. He reminded me of a communist enjoying what he knows is a demonstration trial of an alleged Trotskyist accused of being a fascist agent.

There were moments during the interrogation when I thought of the Moscow trials, and what it must have been like to be a defendant. Suppose Joe McCarthy were dictator and I had been trying to undermine his tyranny, and now he had brought me in and accused me of all sorts of heinous and implausible crimes in addition to the single offense of being against him. If there were no way of communicating the truth to the country, might not a man "confess" to the most wicked absurdities and the most fanciful charges in the hope that people would detect the burlesque?

Fortunately McCarthy was not a dictator; one could leave his hearing room and speak freely outside. So I told the truth and hoped the record would be the answer.

We had gotten now to the point where, under the friendly questioning of Senator Jackson, I was describing the editorial policy of the *Post*.

"I became editor of the *Post* in May, 1949. At that time one of the great issues which the communists were fighting in America was the Marshall Plan. I was a vigorous supporter of the Marshall Plan, and of the Truman Doctrine. These are matters that are on the record. I would be happy to submit to this committee every editorial written since I became editor."

McCarthy remarked dourly: "I do not think that I would care to read them."

For the record I suggested that anyone who rendered such harsh judgment ought to be interested in the written evidence.

McCarthy responded quickly:

"I read enough of your stuff, Mr. Wechsler, to find that your paper, so far as I know, always leads the vanguard, with the *Daily Worker* following the same line, against anyone who is willing to expose communists in Government. That may be your way of fighting communism. Now, you have a perfect right to. People have a right to buy the sheet. I do not care to read any more of it myself. I want to thank you for the invitation, however."

That morning, before I left home, Nancy had admonished me to keep my temper, a plea I have not always heeded. Now, I must confess, I was rather impressed with my demeanor. I asked to introduce a series of additional exhibits, including the chapter from my biography of John L. Lewis dealing with his relations with the communists, my statement of resignation when I left *PM* and the attacks on me published by the *Daily Worker* while I was on *PM*.

The chairman admitted the exhibits and then, in a tone of simulated objectivity, as though talking about someone a thousand miles away, he said:

"Mr. Wechsler, let me ask you this. If you or I were a member of the Communist Party and we wanted to advance the communist cause, perhaps the most effective way of doing that would be to claim that we deserted the party and, if we got in control of the paper, use that paper to attack and smear anybody who actually was fighting communism. Now, without saying whether you have done it, you would agree that would be a good tactic, would you not?"

I replied that I doubted very much that this was one of the stratagems used by the communists. I questioned, for example, whether the presence of Rushmore as a staff member of his committee conclusively proved that the communists had successfully infiltrated the McCarthy operation.

At this point Senator Jackson expressed surprise that there was an ex-communist on the staff, and McCarthy hastened to explain that Rushmore was a very different breed of former communist because he had repeatedly volunteered to testify before congressional committees. Howard, in short, had won his varsity M.

"Rushmore does not spend his time, you see, trying to smear and tear down the people who are really fighting communism," McCarthy said, while Howard tried not to beam.

The chairman let me comment on the point: "Senator, let's face it. You are saying that an ex-communist who is for McCarthy is a good one and an ex-communist who is against McCarthy is a suspect. I will stand on that distinction."

That was incorrect, said McCarthy. The true test of an ex-communist was how many of his former associates he helped to expose. And so we were back there again; the yardstick of an ex-communist's virtue was how big a story he had to tell.

For the record, again, I found myself pointing out that I refused to view ex--communists as a monolithic group. I had defended Whittaker Chambers against the loathsome smears directed at him during the Hiss case; but no obligation of former comradeship required me to swear that Louis Budenz was a scholar or a journalist.

We roved again and then McCarthy returned to what was supposed to have been the subject of the inquiry.

"Do you feel that a committee such as this has the right to and duty to check the books by communist authors on the Information Program shelves?" he asked.

"Sir, I believe that the expedition of your associates was one of the most absurd and fantastic wastes of taxpayers' money in history," I replied. "I do not believe that the presence of one book on one shelf is going to be a decisive issue in the battle against communist ideas. The New York *Post* has not been alone in suggesting that the journey did more to enable the communists to ridicule us than anything that has happened in years."

While I was saying this Cohn smiled fatuously, as if to prove he was a good fellow accustomed to such unfair comment, and Schine, whose resemblance to a vacant-eyed band leader has been discerningly noted by Richard Rovere, seemed to be staring into space, as though trying to recall an old tune.

"Will you get back to my question?" asked McCarthy, employing his favorite phrase.

Throughout the interrogation the grand inquisitor was by turns truculent, contemptuous and bland. Yet I rarely had any feeling of authentic personal animosity. He acted like the gangster in a B-movie who faces the unpleasant necessity of rubbing out someone who has gotten in his way: he would really like the victim to feel that there is nothing personal about it and that he rather regrets the exorbitant demands of duty. At no time did I have the feeling that I was confronted by a fanatic. McCarthy is a poker player, not a zealot, a cold-blooded operator in a big game. There were a few off-the-record asides when he almost seemed to be saying: "Look, don't get excited, old man, we've all got our rackets." This detachment may be his greatest strength; at moments it endows him with a certain cold charm.

When I challenged him sharply, he sometimes assumed the pose of a stern schoolmaster, but even then there seemed to be an element of play-acting. He seemed to enjoy my references to him, as though he at last found my words interesting because they concerned the only truly interesting subject on earth. I am sure some lunatics on the rightist fringe genuinely consider me subversive; at no time did I believe that McCarthy was overcome by that theory. I think he is one of the least passionate demagogues I have ever encountered. I am certain that he would have been happy to shake my hand and forget the whole thing if I had merely indicated that I had misjudged him and was prepared henceforth to write kinder things about him.

What I could not quite determine was whether Roy Cohn had achieved an equivalent cynicism at the age of twenty-six or whether he really believed he was saving the republic. He seemed rather out of things anyway.

It looked as though we were nearing the end.

"As I recall, and I may misquote this, because I do not read your sheet," McCarthy said, "I understand that you have been disturbed by the unfair treatment witnesses received before this committee. Do you feel you were unfairly treated?"

He asked the question almost clinically, like a doctor asking a patient whether the needle he had just administered was really painful.

"Senator, I question the basic nature of this proceeding, of course I do," I replied.

"You feel you were unfairly treated?"

"I regard this proceeding as the first in a long line of attempts to intimidate editors who do not equate McCarthyism with patriotism."

Again he betrayed no resentment over the used of the word "McCarthyism"; I think he is rather proud to be an ism as well as a Senator.

"You have not been intimidated, have you?" he persisted.

"Senator, I am a pretty tough guy," I responded with a certain vanity.

"I say you have not been intimidated, have you?"

"I say this is the first of a long line of attempts to do so," I answered.

"Answer my question. Have you been intimidated?"

"You are not going to win this argument, Senator. We will go back and forth all afternoon."

It was getting to be a comic colloquy, but he wasn't smiling. He seemed genuinely absorbed in the line of questioning. I think one of his true delights is the constant rediscovery of his own strength. For public purposes he may have wanted to wrest a statement that I had not been terrorized, yet I think he would have been equally happy to hear me say that I had been.

"Have you been intimidated?" he repeated in the same phlegmatically insistent voice.

"Sir, I have been taken away from my work. I have not even had a chance to write a word about Senator McCarthy today."

He smiled then; the picture of anyone writing about him could not be unattractive. He hammered back:

"You have not been intimidated at all, have you? You mean you have been inconvenienced. The question is: "Have you been intimidated?"

He was provoking me into a speech.

"I am fully aware this is a proceeding designed to smear the New York *Post*," I said. "I recognize that, Senator. We are both grown up. But this is a free country and I am going to keep fighting.".

"So will the *Daily Worker* and every other communist-line paper," he responded. "But have you been intimidated?"

"I am afraid that is a question we would have to discuss with doctors and get all sorts of expert testimony."

"In other words, you cannot answer that question?"

It was like being a small child and having the town bully ask you whether you have had enough. No answer you can give him is satisfactory to yourself; for if you say that you haven't been frightened, you may re-enforce his sense of virtue, and if you say that you have been he can walk away triumphant. So I clung to the evasive answer.

"I say there is no doubt that this is an attempt to intimidate me. I trust that I have the moral courage to stand up under it. I trust that other editors will."

He would not let go.

"Do you feel that you may have been intimidated? Is there a doubt in your mind as to whether you have been intimidated?"

"We will not know, Senator, until we see whether as editor of the *Post* I keep on fighting just as hard for the things I believe as I have been. I think I will."

"Do you think you have been intimidated?" he asked monotonously.

"I have great confidence in myself, so at the moment, Senator, I feel I have not been intimidated."

"Do you feel you have been abused?"

"Why of course I have been abused. The suggestion that my break with communism was not authentic is the greatest affront you could recite anywhere. I have fought this battle a long time, longer than you have, Senator, and I have taken plenty of beatings from the communists in the course of that fight. So I feel very strongly about this."

Now he spoke in the accents of a judge who, having listened to the devastating words of the prosecutor, delivers his verdict:

"I may say, so that there is no doubt in your mind, so that you need not say that Senator McCarthy intimated or insinuated that you have not broken: I have been following your record, not as closely perhaps as I would if you were in Government, but I have been following you somewhat. I am convinced that you have done exactly what you would do if you were a member of the Communist Party, if you wanted to have a phony break and then use that phony break to the advantage of the Communist Party. I feel that you have not broken with Communist ideals. I feel that you are serving them very, very actively. Whether you are doing it knowingly or not, that is in your own mind. I have no knowledge as to whether you have a card in the party."

I had vowed not to explode; I said as derisively as I could:

"I appreciate that concession."

He ignored the sarcasm; he was very much the judge now, handing down the decision in favor of the prosecutor (who happened to be himself) and untroubled by any murmuring in the courtroom.

"I think you are doing tremendous damage to America," he continued, "when I find books by authors like yourself being purchased by the Information Program we are going to check into them. I say this so you need not say that McCarthy intimated or insinuated. McCarthy did not intimate, he said that he thinks Wechsler is still very, very valuable to the Communist Party."

He was shuffling the papers in front of him and getting ready to depart. My own peroration was inadequate.

"Senator, I should like to say before you leave that under the standards you have established here this afternoon, the only way that I could in your view prove my devotion to America and the validity of my break with communism would be to come out in support of Senator McCarthy. This I do not plan to do."

He was on his feet, his face preoccupied. He was a man who had much more justice to mete out before the day was done and who regarded the present defendant as belonging to the past.

"That I am not asking you to do," he said. "If you ever did that, I would be worried about myself."

Then he walked out.

For the record I delivered a last statement:

"Just one further thing. The *Post* has been fighting Senator McCarthy for a long time. Our editorial page, I am happy to say, has never wavered on this point. It is not going to change now. . . . I answered freely here today because I do not believe that I have anything to hide or that the *Post* has anything to hide.

"I regard this inquiry as a clear invasion of what used to be considered the newspaper's right to act and function independently. I am hopeful that there will be voices raised by newspapers throughout the country in protest against this inquiry, but I repeat again that, rather than give Senator McCarthy the opportunity to distort my stand . . . I have answered all questions to the best of my knowledge and recollection."

There was a perfunctory aftermath. Senator Jackson asked me a few additional questions that enabled me to introduce the remaining exhibits I had brought with me. Roy Cohn got around to asking me about Reed Harris, and I gave the unsatisfactory answer he had anticipated; anything I had to say about Harris was favorable, and Cohn didn't labor the inquiry.

With McCarthy gone the spirit had left the hearing. To debate with Roy Cohn appeared to be the climactic foolishness of the fantastic afternoon. Senator Jackson did not need additional documentation. His problem was how to deal with Joe McCarthy.

It was all over at 5:40, ninety minutes after we had begun.

When we got outside the reporters were there. I told them as accurately as I could the substance of what had occurred and said I would ask that a transcript of the hearing be made public. I also said I would ask the American Society of Newspaper Editors to study the document, since it seemed clear that I have been questioned, not as the author of some undesignated book found in some library overseas, but as the editor of a newspaper that had been fighting Joe McCarthy.

I was dead tired; no ordeal is more exacting that the systematic suppression of one's temper. And there was also an element of despair. Often the communists had said democratic debate is a sham because reaction owns all the weapons. I was too old to believe that nonsense. But for a moment I had to fight the awful fear that this was the century of the demagogues, and that only eighteenth-century romantics could believe that truth always triumphs in the end.

Chapter 4 McCARTHY AND HIS EVIDENCE

One of conservatism's most articulate
spokesmen is WILLIAM F. BUCKLEY, JR.
(b. 1925). In addition to being editor of *National Review*, he writes a syndicated newspaper column, hosts a weekly television
program, and debates and lectures throughout
the country. In recent years he has become a
distinguished novelist: L. BRENT BOZELL
(b. 1925) is an attorney, writer, and editor.
His book *Mustard Seeds: A Conservative Becomes A Catholic* was published in 1986.
Both men deeply admired Senator McCarthy,
and here they defend his aims and tactics.
What was the pattern McCarthy's attacks followed? In what respects were the Senator's
methods "revolutionary"?

It is certainly not characteristic of McCarthy to come forward with dispassionate
recitations of the facts. Rather, like an attorney summing up his case for the jury,
McCarthy emerges as an *interpreter* of the facts: he assumes the role of the government advocate.

McCarthy, characteristically, seizes upon information that tends to point to
disloyalty on the part of a government employee, raises the broad issue of the
employee's loyalty, and makes certain charges against the employee—i.e., he charac-
terizes the employee as a "loyalty risk," as a "pro-Communist," as the "pioneer of
the smear campaign against Chiang Kai-shek," or what have you. McCarthy's critics
insist that it is a part of his method to do all these things without sufficient
evidence to back him up. They insist, that is to say, that in almost every instance

From William F. Buckley, Jr. and L. Brent Bozell, *McCarthy and His Enemies* (Chicago: Henry
Regnery Company, Publishers, 1954), pp. 270-281. Footnotes omitted.

McCarthy has insufficient factual data, either to call into question the employee's loyalty, or to justify his particular characterization of the employee. Thus they conclude that he "smears innocent people."

We propose to survey McCarthy's record with a view to answering these two questions: Does the evidence he presents justify him (a) in raising the loyalty issue, and (b) in using the particular words that he uses in making his charges? Let us, however, be very clear as to why these are different questions, and why they both need to be asked.

To be sure, McCarthy does not commit separately the two sins with which he is charged. Obviously he does not accuse an employee of being a "pro-Communist" without at the same time (directly or indirectly) raising the question of the employee's loyalty. But clearly, while in certain situations McCarthy ought to be censured for having used certain words in describing his target, he may nevertheless have been justified in raising the question whether his target is a loyalty risk.

McCarthy's friends may feel we are wasting time in fastidiously recording the precise language in which McCarthy couches his charges. After all, they will say, the particular words that McCarthy used do not, anyway, stick in the public's mind; the public recalls merely that a man's allegiance has been called into question. So why hold him to account for the exact wording of his accusations? And, as a matter of fact, McCarthy's most violent critics appear to take precisely this position—except, of course, where it turns out that McCarthy has a particularly good case, in which event they hold McCarthy to the exact phrase he used. (For example, after Owen Lattimore was clearly shown to be at best a loyalty risk, they would not let McCarthy forget that he had called Lattimore "the top Soviet espionage agent," not simply a "loyalty risk.") For the most part, however Liberal talk about "smearing" focuses not so much on McCarthy's language as on the contention that, however he happens to phrase it, McCarthy manages to put a person's good name under a cloud, and this on the basis of insufficient evidence. Be that as it may, we intend to analyze McCarthy's method under both tests, harkening again to Lord Acton's counsel that one should try to make out for one's opponents an even stronger and more impressive case than they present themselves.

But before we do this, a word needs to be said about two other fashionable tests by which we are invited to judge the sufficiency of McCarthy's evidence. What might be called the *absolute* test of whether McCarthy has "smeared" people is proposed by the Liberal's question: Is there a discrepancy between what a man has actually done, or what a man has actually thought, and what McCarthy has charged that man with having done or having thought? If this test could be applied, it would surely be the final word as to whether a "smear" has been levelled; but it is obviously unserviceable for purposes of evaluating the charge that a man is pro-Communist. In most other situations the test is indeed servicable, and of course advisable. If, for example, a man is charged with being a member of the Americans for Democratic Action, we can tell whether a smear has been born simply by finding out whether he *is* a member of the Americans for Democratic Action; and this we can do easily enough because members of the ADA do not, as a rule, conceal their membership. But one of the Communist movement's greatest single strengths lies in the skill and determination with which it *prevents* society from finding out which citizens are loyal Communists, and thus disloyal citizens. Thus it becomes very difficult indeed to determine whether X, in calling Y a Communist, has smeared him. The best we can do in the circumstances is to ask whether the charge (by which we mean both the specific accusation and the general impugnation of the person's loyalty) *is justified in the light of necessarily circumstantial evidence.*

In addition to the "absolute proof" test, we must reject what might be called the "legal sufficiency" test. Many of McCarthy's critics are given to pointing out that his evidence in nearly every case is insufficient to establish that the accused has broken the law, which is usually true. But they are also given to saying that this is evidence of McCarthy's irresponsibility, which is foolishness. Only in the rare exception does McCarthy even *accuse* his targets of having broken the law. But he does insist, as a general thing, that the evidence he offers is sufficient to warrant the dismissal of his targets from government service. Thus, those who quarrel with McCarthy on this score (taking the position that only proven lawbreakers should be dismissed from the government) should address their grievances to those who drafted the rules for government employment—not to McCarthy, who merely plays by these rules. For by 1947, at the very latest, Congress and both political parties had explicitly endorsed the notion that government service is a privilege, not a right; and that therefore government personnel must meet standards a good deal more exacting than those set forth in the criminal code. Job security for civil servants was therefore to depend not only on their staying outside the law's reach, but also on their satisfying their superiors that their employment was in the national interest.

All this appears to be obvious; but it apparently is not, else we would not hear, so frequently, that McCarthy is to be damned because he goes after government employees without adhering to the standards of proof required of a district attorney going after a thief.

Let us go on now with a review of McCarthy's record, keeping in mind the two questions: Is the evidence he presents sufficient, typically, to justify what McCarthy says about his targets? And is it sufficient, typically, to warrant his calling their loyalty into question?

On the whole, McCarthy's attacks have followed a pattern. Most often he has gone after government employees, or former government employees. If the target of his attack is still employed, McCarthy calls for his dismissal. If he is no longer employed, he calls for an investigation of the security agency of the Department in which he worked. If he finds the employee has not even been processed (which is often the case), he lets the world know that he is flabbergasted. If he finds the employee has been processed and cleared (which is also often the case), he also lets the world know that he is flabbergasted.

McCarthy's critics have so effectively popularized the notion that McCarthy smears a half dozen Americans every week that the statistics may be surprising: The Grand Inquisitor of the Twentieth Century has publicly accused, as of questionable loyalty or reliability, a total of 46 persons. Of these 46, McCarthy mentioned twelve only once, and then only to point that their security status was pending in the State Department and that eleven of them had nevertheless not been suspended from their work.

With respect to ten others, McCarthy merely quoted from derogatory reports developed by other investigators, with a view to persuading the Senate that least a *prima facie* case existed for questioning the operating standards of a loyalty program that had cleared them. With one exception (Remington), little public attention was given to these ten. They do not, in short, classify as "McCarthy cases" for purposes of shedding light on this method.

It is, consequently, on the basis of charges against twenty-four persons, whose cases he has especially dramatized, that McCarthy has earned his reputation as "a wholesale poisoner, a perverted destroyer of innocent reputations."

To get down to cases: McCarthy has never said anything more damaging about Lauchlin Currie, Gustavo Duran, Theodore Geiger, Mary Jane Keeney, Edward Posniak, Haldore Hanson, and John Carter Vincent, than that they are known to one or more responsible persons as having been members of the Communist Party, which is in each of these instances true. The fact that this charge against Hanson and Vincent is underwritten exclusively by Louis Budenz is not the basis of legitimate criticism of McCarthy; he cannot be called a smearer because he chooses to rely on the integrity of Budenz. Nor is McCarthy guilty of reckless character assassination because he chooses to take the word of the Spanish Government as against Gustavo Duran's; nor because he finds the testimony of the FBI undercover agents on Posniak's membership in the Party more persuasive than Posniak's denials. Mr. Robert Morris, assistant counsel for the Tydings Committee, offered to present to the Committee "some witnesses . . . who will testify that [Theodore Geiger] . . . was a member of the same Communist Party unit as they were. . . ." Elizabeth Bentley has testified that Lauchlin Currie was a member of a Soviet apparatus. Mary Jane Keeney, having been named as acting as a Communist courier, was dismissed from her post with the United Nations after adverse loyalty reports on her were submitted by the State Department, and has since been cited for contempt by the Internal Security Committee of the Senate.

In short, McCarthy cannot, in our opinion, be indicted as a character assassin for circulating the above facts and for turning them into an accusation against the person concerned. And it readily follows that, in the light of such data, he was fully entitled to call their loyalty into question.

Lattimore has been identified as a member of the Communist Party by Louis

Budenz, and as a member of Russian Military Intelligency by Alexander Barmine; and the McCarran Committee classified him, in a unanimous report, as a "conscious articulate instrument of the Soviet conspiracy." There can be no denying, then, that McCarthy was justified in calling Lattimore's loyalty into question.

But McCarthy's specific charges against Lattimore went a good deal further than publication of the evidence that was available; and for this exaggeration he is indeed censurable. He told the Tydings Committee (in executive session, to be sure) that Lattimore was the "top Soviet espionage agent in America"–a daring allegation in the light of our notorious ignorance of the hierarchy of the Soviet espionage apparatus. A few days later, McCarthy modified this charge, in a speech from the Senate floor.

(It was not McCarthy, one must remember, who publicized Lattimore as the "top American espionage agent"; Drew Pearson broke the story that McCarthy had so described Lattimore in a *closed* session of the Tydings Committee. It was thus a friend and admirer of Lattimore who set in motion Lattimore's "ordeal by slander.")

Though McCarthy's exaggeration is deplorable, it can hardly be maintained that it has been responsible for severely damaging Lattimore. Our society (as distinct from our laws) does not appear to attach more importance to the distinction between membership in the Party, and espionage in behalf of the Party. J. Peters is not more despised an American than Frederick Vanderbilt Field.

To return to the instances in which McCarthy did *not* misinterpret or exaggerate: McCarthy's insistence that John Stewart Service was a loyalty risk is supported in every respect. Service *was* named by General Hurley as a member of the State Department cabal that was attempting to undermine Hurley's influence in China and urging a policy essentially pro-Chinese-Communist. And Service *was* arrested by the FBI on charges of releasing classified material to unauthorized persons. Nor is that all: the Civil Service Loyalty Review Board ultimately concurred in McCarthy's judgment–to the extent, at least, of ruling that there was a "reasonable doubt" as to Service's loyalty.

Thus it cannot be said that McCarthy smeared Service either in the way he framed the charges against him or in the fact that he called into question Service's loyalty.

The same verdict holds with respect to Professors Schuman and Shapely. McCarthy merely accused them of inveterate party-lining and Communist-fronting. Of these activities they were unqualifiedly guilty. . . .

Of William T. Stone, McCarthy has said that his "Communist activities are legion." What McCarthy refers to is set down in a previous chapter. An extremely cautious man might have said "dubious" instead of "Communist." But let us remember that the State Department security office, after studying Stone's record as far back as March, 1946, had recommended that "action be instituted to terminate his services with the State Department immediately." Held to strictest account for the phraseology of his charge, McCarthy probably "smeared" Stone; but if he did, he smeared a man who through the years had taken little pains to protect himself from such charges as were levelled against him. As for the second question we are asking (was McCarthy entitled to call Stone's loyalty into question?), the Department security division's own recommendation provides the obvious answer: Yes.

John Paton Davies has been a target of McCarthy ever since 1950. McCarthy quoted General Hurley as having accused Davies of encouraging, behind his back, a policy favorable to the Chinese Communists. "Davies has been suitably rewarded by Dean Acheson for his sell-out of an ally," said McCarthy to the Senate. "Davies is now . . . in Washington as a member of the State Department's Policy Planning Committee, where he is strategically placed to help further the betrayal he began in Chungking." Hard talk, certainly. But "betrayal" is a word that American political lingo was using generously long before McCarthy appeared; and we cannot demand of McCarthy greater verbal precision than is considered par in his metier. But we must not beg the question: McCarthy unquestionably considers Davies a security risk. He is at least not alone in questioning Davies' reliability; the McCarran Committee found that Davies "testified falsely" on a matter "substantial in import" (i.e., concerning his alleged recommendations that the CIA retain certain persons known to be Communists). We do not believe, therefore, that either McCarthy's specific charges against Davies or his calling Davies' loyalty into question were unreasonable.

McCarthy's charges against Philip Jessup, Dorothy Kenyon and Esther Brunauer have been treated amply in the chapter on the Tydings Committee, where we reached the conclusion that McCarthy was justified in bringing their names into a loyalty probe. However, we also saw there that, in the Jessup and Kenyon cases, McCarthy was guilty, in two instances, of gratuitous sensationalism—e.g., his singling Jessup out as the "pioneer" of the anti-Chiang conspiracy, and his calling Miss Kenyon's Communist-front colleagues her "fellow-reds."

Summarizing the security file on Peveril Meigs, McCarthy said in February, 1950, "So far as I know, everything in this individual's file indicates that he is actively working with and for the Communists." Whether this is so, and therefore whether McCarthy is guilty of having smeared Meigs, we do not know, not having had access to the file in question. It is public knowledge, however, that subsequent to McCarthy's charges against Meigs, he was discharged from the Army under the loyalty program. Therefore, the presumption is that McCarthy's questioning of Meigs' loyalty was reasonable.

Drew Pearson definitely *was* smeared by McCarthy on both counts; and the only defense McCarthy could possibly make (which we do not propose to encourage) would run in such terms as, "Those who live by the smear shall perish by the smear." . . .

This then, is McCarthy's record. As regards one of the two fundamental questions we have been asking (are McCarthy's specific charges warranted in the light of his evidence?), it is clear that he has been guilty of a number of exaggerations, some of them reckless; and perhaps some of them have unjustly damaged the persons concerned beyond the mere questioning of their loyalty. For these transgressions we have neither the desire to defend him nor the means to do so. Measured against the moral command that prescribes every witting divergence from the truth, they are reprehensible. It remains only to be said that *McCarthy's record is nevertheless not only much better than his critics allege but, given his metier, extremely good.*

As regards the other standard for determining whether smearing has been a characteristic of McCarthy's method (Does the evidence McCarthy presents justify calling into question his targets' loyalty?), the case-by-case breakdown clearly renders a verdict extremely favorable to McCarthy. With the two exceptions of Drew Pearson and George Marshall, not a single person was accused by McCarthy whose loyalty could not be questioned on the basis of a most responsible reading of official records. And this is the only test that seems to be relevant for deciding whether McCarthy "habitually smears people." When a man's loyalty is questioned, more often than not it makes little difference to him just *how* and in what terms it is questioned.

We may be wrong. But if we *are* right in insisting that this is the apter test, then the record clearly exonerates McCarthy of "habitual character assassination" and of "smearing of innocent people."

"Character assassination" is, of course, a part of McCarthy's method only if we so choose to call the exposure of past activities and associations of government employees. McCarthy has tirelessly combed the records of public servants; and, when the evidence has warranted it, and Administration intransigence blocked other alternatives, he has publicly disclosed their past activities and associations and has raised the question whether, given their records, they merit public confidence. His concern has not been with establishing "guilt," but with seeing to it that security personnel apply standards stringent enough to give this country the protection it needs against well-camouflaged Communists.

The role of public prosecutor is never an enviable one. His competence is usually judged, unfortunately, on the basis of the number of convictions he wins. The counterpart of the public prosecutor in the security field cannot hope for such clean-cut vindications. At most he succeeds in persuading the "jury"—the Loyalty Security Board—that the doubt as to Jones' loyalty or reliability is "reasonable." And even then, he must face the vituperation of those who not only deem the doubt *un*reasonable, but openly challenge the competence of *any* tribunal to adjudicate such a question.

Let us remember in this connection that it is never particularly difficult to offer a plausible explanation or defense for any stand—or association—that raises doubts as to loyalty or reliability. How often we find ourselves sympathizing, spontaneously and warm-heartedly, with the witness who accounts for his participation in a Communist front in terms of a deeply felt identification with the humanitarian objectives with which that front was ostensibly concerned. And how often we fail to remind ourselves that, if the organization was in *fact* a Communist front, *somebody* concerned with it wasn't so much concerned with social reform as with furthering the interests of the Soviet Union, and that therefore the function of security agencies is precisely to look skeptically at explanations commonly accepted as plausible. The layman is perhaps entitled to accept the accounting of the frontjoiner, and to despise the "morbid" suspiciousness of the person who does not accept it. But *not* the security agencies—and *not* a United States Senator who feels a vocation to see to it that they do their job. For the hard fact of the matter is that the suspicious person may be the worse person. And because of bitter experience, we have adopted a national security policy which instructs security personnel to *be* suspicious, and to find against the individual if so much as a reasonable *doubt* exists as to his reliability.

The case of John Stewart Service, if we may drag it up again, illustrates the problem. McCarthy has been severely castigated for imputing disloyalty to a man "whose only crime has been bad judgment." Service, an experienced China hand, dispatched from the field report upon report to his superiors in the Department of State. These reports are of such character as to discredit the hypothesis that their author was both (a) a shrewd reporter, familiar with China, and (b) an anti-Communist. Two alternative hypotheses suggest themselves: (a) Service is not a shrewd reporter; i.e., he is congenitally naive, or else he was temporarily bamboozled; or (b) he was shrewd but not an anti-Communist. The first explanation is the more attractive, but the second is not unthinkable. Then, on top of it all, John Service gets himself arrested by the FBI for turning over classified information to unauthorized persons who, as it happened, were Communists. Two explanations again arise: (a) Service did not deem the information to be in any way critical, and hence he granted himself the authority to reclassify classified information (sometimes exercised by public servants); or (b) Service *wished* to supply the Communists with information to which they might not otherwise have access. Either explanation could account for Service's action. But in the context of an international emergency, McCarthy steps forward to argue that there is at the very least *a reasonable doubt* of Service's loyalty, and that the State Department should therefore dismiss him. McCarthy was perhaps not acting generously, but he certainly was acting reasonably.

This, then, is "McCarthy's method." Notwithstanding the hectically promoted public impression, McCarthy does not make a practice of fabricating evidence. He does, however, make a practice of acting on the proposition—on which he insists the government also act—that Alger Hiss was not the last of the Soviet agents in our midst, and that Hiss' comrades do not publicly parade their allegiance to the Soviet Union.

We have likened McCarthy's role to that of the prosecutor; but let us keep in mind the hazards of carrying the analogy too far. The greatest psychological propaganda victory the Communist and the Liberals have scored in this whole area has been to force everyone to discuss the loyalty-security issue in the terminology of law. The authors of this book are themselves guilty of having used, in the preceding pages, the organically inappropriate imagery of the law, because otherwise they could not join issue with the opposition. But it is palpably foolish to speak, in the area of government security, of "defendant" and "prosecutor," of "guilt" and "innocence," of "proof," of the "presumption of innocence," of the "right to confront one's accuser," of the "right to cross-examination," of "judgement by one's peers," and the rest of it. So long as we continue to use this terminology we can hardly hope to understand the problem at hand, much less to cope with it. We have, in fact, understood and coped with it just to the extent that we have fought ourselves free, at some points, from the legal imagery and its misleading implications.

It is all to the good that we make the district attorney respect the rights of the accused and depend, for a verdict of "guilty," upon the unanimous approval of the jury. Only at our peril do we abandon such revered customs. But let us not be deceived by certain similarities between the role of a public prosecutor and the role of a McCarthy, or between the position of the accused in a murder trial and the position of a Vincent in a security proceeding. The differences between the two are far greater than the similarities, and they reflect all the wisdom we have acquired about how to deal with the Communists in our midst.

The essence of McCarthy—and McCarthyism—lies then in bringing to the loyalty-security problem a kind of skepticism with which it had not been approached before. Others took it for granted that Service backed the Chinese Communists and gave away classified material because he was fooled. McCarthy was prepared to suppose he did so because he was pro-Communist. Others explained Shapley's party-lining in terms of devotion to world peace; McCarthy recognized that devotion to world Communism was an alternative hypothesis that merited equal treatment. And he keeps on being skeptical if, as so often happens, the evidence does not conclusively establish either hypothesis, McCarthy is there to insist that we cannot afford to *act* on any but the hypothesis that favors our national security. McCarthy would unquestionably admit that Service *might* be innocent; but he would never consent to reinstate him in a position of public trust.

This is the heart of McCarthy's method. It is in many respects as revolutionary as the Communist movement itself—and so it is unlikely to commend itself to people so short on knowledge, or even instincts, as to the nature and resources of the Soviet conspiracy as not to realize that we live in an unbrave new world, in which certain cherished habits of mind are not only inappropriate but suicidal.

Chapter 5 HISTORY WILL VINDICATE HIM

One of Joe McCarthy's closest political associates during the heighth and depth of his
career as an investigator was ROY COHN
(1927-1986). In the following excerpt from
his book *McCarthy*, published in 1968, the
controversial New York attorney weighs the
Senator's goals and techniques, discusses
the nature of his opposition, and depicts
McCarthy as a champion of First Amendment
rights. Predictably, Cohn argues that his former employer was an effective opponent of
Communists and "pro-Communists."

It would be instructive to consider in some depth why the critical barrage against
McCarthy was so incessant, so amazingly shrill and so monstrously abusive.

I believe we can dismiss, after reflection, the man's burliness, his impatience, his
aggressiveness, and his refusal to compromise. He was cast for the role of arch-
villain, but these were superficial characteristics hardly calling for such violent
abuse. Moreover, he was not the only public figure in history who possessed such
physical attributes as a heavy beard that could easily be caricatured.

We cannot dismiss as easily the charges that he played rough politics, occasionally took unfair advantage of people, and said harsh things in public. McCarthy's
heat-of-battle pronunciations were often unnecessarily strong. His "Alger—I mean
Adlai" reference to Adlai Stevenson was regrettable, and his characterization of the

McCarthy—Copyright 1968 by Roy Cohn; used with permission of the Foley Agency. Pp.
246-252 and 275-279.

Democrats as the "party of treason" was an inexcusably broad (and therefore inaccurate) accusation. These tactics generated understandable antagonism.

But can we ascribe the hate and venom he aroused in many quarters to his campaign conduct? Americans recognize that politics is often a merciless contest. Political abuse is an old American custom. Jefferson the "bastard son of an Indian woman," Lincoln the "drunkard," Grover Cleveland the "lecher," and Andrew Jackson who was given names not fit for the printed page even by today's libertarian standards are rated by American historians as among our greatest presidents. Two others highly regarded, Woodrow Wilson and Franklin Roosevelt, also came in for extraordinary abuse and nasty innuendos. McCarthy's case is almost unique in the history of political slander in that the victim was not a liberal but right of center. . . .

Was he reviled because his enemies feared him as a fanatic, a would-be dictator who wanted to foist a kind of fascism upon the United States? I think here we come a little closer to an answer. There was indeed such a fear, that much the stronger because the nation had just emerged from the bloody struggle with two fascist dictators. But upon further analysis, this explanation doesn't entirely hold up either. Even Rovere, who calls McCarthy a demagogue, ultimately admits that he did not have the soul of a Hitler, was never consumed by dreams of power, and was not a man possessed by demons.

Senator McCarthy knew his influence, but it is far-fetched to accept the mystique that he was a man driven by the need for absolute power over the lives of men and the destinies of nations. He was too cavalier, too disorganized concerning the wisdom of his own political moves, for there to be any substance to this theory. He did not seek his powerful chairmanship; it just happened by operation of the rule of seniority when the Democrats were temporarily dislodged in 1952. Despite the controversy over his use of the power, power for its own sake was never McCarthy's goal. He was politically ambitious, but the same might be said of every seeker after public office.

Many journalists took a dual approach to this charge of fanaticism. Privately, they thought he was an uncommitted crusader who had found a "good thing" that commanded publicity; in print, they sought to discredit him with charges of fanaticism. The truth is that McCarthy was basically a simple man who lacked the burning zeal of the single-track cause-fighter. He was courageous though, and when he became convinced that Communism was an evil, he took up the battle against its inroads into American life and fought the tough way he had learned how to fight early in life.

Why then was McCarthy so feared and hated? I believe there were two basic reasons. The liberal intellectual element in government and the communications media regarded his as a mortal threat; and political leaders, including the conservative Establishment, saw in him and in his "issue" a force that if allowed to carry on would split the Republican party from top to bottom.

McCarthy was the first public figure in a position of practically unchallengeable power to threaten by his activity the freedom, the livelihood, and the social function of liberals, chiefly in the Government. Liberals were and still are in control of large sections of the press, radio, TV, and motion pictures. These people believed that the facts McCarthy was digging after could, if carried to their logical conclusion, directly threaten them. Their own transgressions, stupidities, or mere indiscretions magnified by exposure and publicity would hurt them badly; their protective mechanism resorted to hate and obstruction aimed at the investigator and his allies.

Perhaps the chief reason for the distrust and scorn of certain elements of the rank and file was their acceptance of the image of McCarthy as a bully who habitually indulged, from a safe and entrenched position, in no-quarter attacks on vulnerable persons he seemed to have accused and condemned almost before they had sat down to be questioned. Such was the impression emanating from many newspapers and from radio and TV sets. He appeared to be running amok, with no one on the horizon to stop him. American political history had no precedent for his kind of attack before such a huge watching and reading public.

The juggernaut progress of this Irish bull seemed to pose a special problem for the Jewish community. Jews are numerous in the various branches of the communications industry. They had a special memory, and a long one, of persecution. Many had been led politically leftward by the terrifying rise of Hitler and they had a feeling of gratitude toward the Soviet Union for its major role in toppling the Nazis.

These factors along with the ever-present Jewish concern for civil liberties account for the opposition (often unreasonable in my opinion) of many Jews and Jewish organizations to anti-Communism. In my opinion they rendered a disservice to the Jewish community because they fostered the impression that there was a mystic link between Judaism and Communism. Such an idea is, of course, ridiculous, since Judaism's great historical contribution is a moral God, while Communism's crusade is for atheism.

Instead of excusing leftist causes, certain Jewish organizations would have done better had they pointed out the inconsistencies between Judaism and Communism, and the mistreatment of Jews in the Soviet Union. Instead of defending morally indefensible people (some of whom happened to be Jews) involved in Communist activity, they should have praised the many Jews in the forefront of the fight against Communism. While it is true that the Rosenbergs were Jewish, so too were those who prosecuted them, such as Irving H. Saypol, the competent and vigorous United States attorney (now state supreme court justice). And so is Federal Judge Irving R. Kaufman (since elevated to the United States Court of Appeals), whose conduct of the trial was so fair that even the Rosenbergs' lawyer praised it. American boys of Jewish faith died fighting for freedom in Korea and in Vietnam. The staunch Americanism of such Jews as presidential adviser Bernard Baruch, Admiral Hyman Rickover, the distinguished lawyer Edwin L. Weisl, who while serving as chief counsel to the Senate Preparedness Committee fashioned the space act, Rabbi Joshua Goldberg, militant foe of Communism and Jewish chaplin for the United States Navy—these are only a few of the names that spring to mind. The mishandling of this Communist issue by some Jewish organizations resulted in the creation of the American Jewish League against Communism by a group of prominent American Jews including George Sokolsky, Eugene Lyons, and Alfred Kohlberg. As J. Edgar Hoover pointed out in his book *Masters of Deceit,* this League was "the first American organization to expose and document the Communist anti-Jewish policies." Russia bans the teaching of Hebrew, forbids Jews to visit Israel, and has barred Jews from positions of importance in the country. No Jewish publication may be issued.

McCarthy was the first important public figure to touch an exquisitely sensitive nerve in the thought leaders of our society. This small but immensely powerful group of intellectuals is committed totally to the idea of an open society, in which there is no officially accepted truth, no dogma handed down by authority and believed without question. Their leaders believe with John Stuart Mill that in a political society "there ought to exist the fullest liberty of prefessing and discussing, as a matter of ethical conviction, any doctrine, however immoral it may be considered." Thus the way to get at a truth is to have an open market of ideas, and the successful contender in the marketplace could be identified as the political truth—for the time being. Of course, the truth can change if a new contender should arise and displace it.

For this thesis to be implemented, it must follow that society can place no obstructions in the path of a full exploration of any new candidate for truth that may come along. Thus contemporary liberalism holds that it is the worst of sins to punish anybody for the advocacy of a competing idea. One must be left free to thoroughly examine any idea that comes along.

Doctrinaire liberals were angered when legislation designed to combat subversive activities was debated and enacted. They did not favor a law that ordered all agents of foreign governments to register with the Department of Justice (the McCormack Act of 1938), or a law barring from Federal employment any member of an organization that advocates the overthrow of the United States Government by force of violence (the Hatch Act of 1939), or a law punishing those who would advocate the forceful overthrow of this Government (the Smith Act of 1940). They did not like these laws, but neither did they quiver with fear and hate. Theirs was at least controlled hostility.

Now along came Senator Joseph McCarthy. And he came, these liberal leaders believed, with another kind of idea. McCarthy, they convinced themselves, was telling the nation that it was not enough to pass laws protecting ourselves from these outside dangers. We must excommunicate not only the *individual* from our society but also the *ideas* he espouses. And it was here that the liberals became alarmed and then enraged. The notion that any idea whatever, no matter how bizarre, how revolutionary, how dangerous in political effect, can be ruled out of the forum jarred the deepest commitment of the liberal community.

Professor Willmoore Kendall, in his book *The Conservative Affirmation,* develops this thesis that McCarthy was hated because he was the spokesman for a large group that would enforce a public orthodoxy—set up a code of officially accepted beliefs in this country, expunging ideas they believed immoral or which threatened our society's survival. His theory is enormously interesting, but he did not really know McCarthy.

The truth is simply that McCarthy embraced no such philosophy, or in fact any world-view whatsoever. He was no political thinker, no innovator. He was the enemy not of free speech but of the abuse of the First Amendment. He would outlaw only the advocacy of force and violence to change our form of government. He did not believe as did Thomas Jefferson in a whimsical moment that a revolution now and then is good for a society. He was rather with Calvin Coolidge and the D.A.R.: "We have had our Revolution." He belonged to the respectable political school (however unorthodox his actions may have been) that Americans are not afraid of ideas or public persuasion but only of espionage, sabotage, and the appeal to a violent change. His test was: after all the talking and debate, put it to the vote and abide by the decision of the majority.

Those whose hatred of McCarthy stemmed from confusing him with the Far Righters, who actually did advocate a patriotic orthodoxy, have a point, a reason for their confusion. The Senator and those on his right were patriots who elevated pride in the Flag to a religion, and regarded antagonists to prayer in the public schools as sneaking atheists and dissent from the war in Korea (or now Vietnam) or the failure to save China from Communism as treason.

In seeing him as the Man on Horseback, the would-be dictator working toward the take-over, they paid Joe McCarthy a tribute he did not deserve. He was a man not consumed by an ideology; one who, like Theodore Roosevelt, "thought with his hips." He was a man of action, but without a comprehensive plan to be President, much less a dictator.

But believing that he threatened the American way of life itself, many citizens found in that an ample justification for a very special hatred. . . .

I was fully aware of McCarthy's faults, which were neither few nor minor. He was impatient, overly aggressive, overly dramatic. He acted on impulse. He tended to sensationalize the evidence he had—in order to draw attention to the rock-bottom seriousness of the situation. He would neglect to do important homework and consequently would, on occasion, make challengeable statements.

His impatience with detail sometimes caused minor explosions at executive sessions of the subcommittee. Much of a senatorial committee's work consists of tedious and often uninteresting detail, so that whenever McCarthy knew that a meeting was to be devoted to ratifications of appointments, promotions, and what he called "office manager stuff" he would deputize an assistant to act for him.

Once, when he could not dodge such a session, I watched him grow more and more irritated. When two senators actually quarreled over the promotion of a girl on the staff, McCarthy banged with an ashtray—he never used a gavel—and shouted: "Look, I'm trying to get my appropriation for the year so that I can get Communists out of Government. I'm not going to sit here all afternoon listening to you two arguing over whether Mary is going up to grade eleven or not. I don't want to hear about it. Fight it out later."

Ultimately, this inattention to detail, this failure to check and recheck every point he made, enabled his enemies to divert attention from the main thrust of his attack to the details—which, in too many cases, did not bear close scrutiny.

But it must be understood that in an important sense McCarthy was a salesman. He was selling the story of America's peril. He knew that he could never hope to convince anybody by delivering a dry, general-accounting-office type of presentation. In consequence, he stepped up circumstances a notch or two.

Did the urgent need to get the story across excuse a broad-brush approach? I can understand why he did it, as I can realize that his dramatizations hurt him in many quarters. I quarreled with him frequently on this score and stressed that by using this technique he sometimes placed himself in an indefensible position. But I never disagreed with the substance of his thesis.

This controversial technique was evident in the very first speech that launched McCarthy upon the great issue of his career. He was planning a nationwide series of talks, beginning at Wheeling, on an explosive subject he hoped would arouse the country. Surely this called for careful advance preparation. The speech should have been written out beforehand and copies distributed. And surely, precise information on the number of individuals concerned was essential. But because the speech was not prepared in advance, and because he really wasn't certain exactly how many persons were Communists and how many security risks, he gave him enemies a perfect opportunity to throw up a screen. Thus the so-called numbers game began.

A great controversy arose after McCarthy's Wheeling speech. McCarthy's critics claimed that whereas he said there that 205 Communists were working in the State Department, later in Reno he whittled the number down to 57. Still later he spoke of "81 cases." They demanded to know what he really meant. Didn't his confusion over the figures reveal that he didn't know what he was talking about?

Eleven days after the Wheeling talk, McCarthy was summoned to explain his charges before a quickly created special committee of the Senate Committee on Foreign Relations, headed by the venerable Maryland Democrat, Millard E. Tydings. The Tydings subcommittee, after taking 1,498 pages of testimony, issued a report calling McCarthy's charges against the State Department a "fraud and a hoax."

Buckley and Bozell, in their analysis of the Tydings episode, state that McCarthy showed himself to be "inexperienced, or, worse still, misinformed. Some of his specific charges were exagerrated; a few had no apparent foundation whatever." Let us accept the fact that McCarthy was unable to offer conclusive evidence that there were "57 card-carrying Communists" in the State Department. Let us accept the fact that McCarthy's material was drawn from a four-year-old letter written by Secretary Byrnes. Let us accept the fact that McCarthy was forced to step nimbly in an effort to explain his figures. He insisted that at Wheeling he referred to 205 persons declared unfit for Government service who were still in the Department, that the 57 referred to Department employees who were either members of the Communist party or loyal to it, that the 81 included the 57, plus additional cases of less importance against whom the evidence was less conclusive.

But let us never forget that the substance of his charges was true. There *were* persons working in the State Department whose activities and associations indicated they had pro-Communist leanings. Could any American rest easily, knowing pro-Communists may have been helping to shape our foreign policy?

McCarthy's broad-brush technique was again illustrated by his charge that the Democratic party was guilty of "twenty years of treason." This is nonsense if taken literally. Frederick Woltman, the late Scripps-Howard journalist, pointed out that this statement pinned the label of traitor on the 26,898,281 Americans who voted the Democratic ticket in 1952.

Certainly McCarthy did not intend the statement to be accepted at face value. He meant to shock, to awaken. He singled out the New Deal era, during which Communism in Government flourished with impunity. This attack on the Democrats made McCarthy many powerful enemies and accounted for the' solid Democratic vote for censure in 1954.

Let us examine McCarthy's attacks on Owen Lattimore, a Johns Hopkins professor, an authority on China's borderlands, and à leading figure in the Institute for Pacific Relations. He had been editor of I.P.R.'s publication, *Pacific Affairs.* The I.P.R. was, on the surface, a scholarly organization collecting and disseminating information about the Far East. In reality, it "was taken over by Communist design and made a vehicle for attempted control of American thinking and American policy with regard to the Far East." This description is from a 1952 report of the Senate Internal Security Committee.

Lattimore had considerable influence over our Far East policies. On President Roosevelt's recommendation Chiang Kai-shek appointed him his personal adviser during 1940. He was deputy director of the OWI overseas branch in 1942 and 1943, and served on the Pauley reparations mission in Japan and Manchuria.

Two years before, McCarthy had told the Tydings Committee at a closed session that Lattimore was "definitely as espionage agent . . . one of the top espionage agents . . . the key man in a Russian espionage ring." The remark was leaked to Drew Pearson, who published it, and an uproar resulted.

When challenged, McCarthy said on the Senate floor: "I fear that I may have perhaps placed too much stress on the question of whether or not he had been an espionage agent. . . ." But he had said, as part of the charge against Lattimore, "I am willing to stand or fall on this one."

A unanimous Senate Internal Security Subcommittee of Democrats and Republicans, including Senator Arthur Watkins, found after hearings that Lattimore "was, from some time beginning in the 1930's, a conscious, articulate instrument of the Soviet conspiracy."

It was never proved that Lattimore was a Soviet espionage agent. Subsequently, an indictment charging perjury was brought against Lattimore, but the Government dropped the case after two key counts were dismissed on technical grounds.

It was in a 72,000-word speech on June 14, 1951, in the Senate (read into the record but not actually given) that Senator McCarthy reviewed the weaknesses he found in the career of General George C. Marshall. The Senator, without any doubt, severely damaged his own image with many Americans when he called Marshall "a man so steeped in falsehood who has recourse to the lie whenever it suits his convenience" and went so far as to suggest that Marshall was some kind of traitor to his country. This was dynamite in the context of Marshall's reputation as a beloved old soldier.

A calmer, more conservative presentation might have gotten across the valid and important point that despite his highly respected military career, Marshall's role in China directly after World War II was disastrous to the interests of the United States—which were to prevent a Communist take-over in that enormous country. Marshall's political naiveté let him fall victim to the then-prevalent line that the Chinese Communists were not a menace, but were merely agrarian reformers interested only in fighting local corruption. History has shown how we were taken in, and Marshall bears a heavy responsibility. But the violent characterization with which Joe emphasized the Marshall role in this disaster dwarfed the issue into comparative insignificance—and battle lines were drawn instead on Marshall's reputation.

Looking back with whatever objectivity I can muster, I believe that even after all the excesses and mistakes are counted up, Senator McCarthy used the best methods available to him to fight a battle that needed to be fought. The methods were far from perfect, but they were not nearly as imperfect as uninformed critics suggest. The use of Executive sessions to protect witnesses from publicity until they had an opportunity to explain adverse evidence; the respect of the constitutional privilege; the right given each witness to have counsel beside him at all times—these compare favorably not only with methods of other investigating committees but with methods of certain prosecutors. The "methods" attack on McCarthy suffers from a credibility gap because of the double standard of many critics, particularly the press, radio, and television. To them, anything McCarthy did was wrong, but the excesses and outrageous methods of those not investigating subversion are often overlooked or excused.

He may have been wrong in details, but he was right in essentials. Certainly few can deny that the Government of the United States had in it enough Communist sympathizers and pro-Soviet advisers to twist and pervert American foreign policy for close to two decades.

He was a man of a peculiar time: the Cold War. His particular "package" would not have been deliverable in the depressed but exhilarating thirties. But he came forward at the time of Communist aggression in Korea and the triumph of Mao's revolution. The job he had to do could hardly have been done by a gentle, tolerant spirit who could see all around a problem.

What is indisputable is that he was a courageous man who fought a monumental evil. He did so against opposition as determined as was his own attack—an opposition that spent far more time, money, and print seeking to expose *him* than Communism.

Since his day, Cuba has fallen to the Communists. The free world was rocked in 1967 by the Harold Philby revelation of Communist infiltration in high Government security posts. Nuclear explosions echo over China and the Soviet Union. American men are defending the borders of South Vietnam against Communist aggressors. North Korea has laid down the gauntlet to us.

Has not history already begun his vindication?

Part Two

McCARTHYISM AND PARTISAN POLITICS

Chapter 6 TRUMAN AND THE RED SCARE

ATHAN THEOHARIS (b. 1936) views
McCarthyism in large part as a direct
product of the Truman Administration.
What specifically might the president have
done to avoid the author's charges? Mr.
Theoharis, one of the small but influential
number of "New Left" scholars, is a
professor of history at Marquette
University. His books include *The Yalta
Myths: An Issue in U.S. Politics, 1945-1955*
and *Spying on Americans: Political
Surveillance from Hoover to the Huston
Plan.*

Popular fears about threats to American national security were far indeed from
being endemic in the United States at the end of World War II. In 1945, according
to opinion polls, most Americans believed that a durable peace required the con-
tinuation of Allied cooperation; thus they welcomed the Yalta Conference as a
means of achieving that objective. Majority opinion supported Roosevelt's efforts
to promote mutual trust and understanding with the Soviet Union; it recognized
the necessity for compromise and appreciated the inevitable differences in purposes
between the "democracies" of the United States, the Soviet Union, and Great
Britain. In 1945 most Americans considered the Soviet Union to be not the Anti-
Christ but a Great Power having legitimate security aims which sometimes con-
flicted with those of the United States. Most differences between the United States

Reprinted by permission of Quadrangle Books from *Seeds of Repression* by Athan Theoharis,
copyright ©1971 by Athan Theoharis. Pp. 29-36, 98-101, and 114-120.

and the Soviet Union were considered resolvable through international conferences—particularly conferences involving the Big Three—and required diplomatic
compromise, not military confrontation.

In line with these views, a popular distrust of the military prevailed. This distrust
was reflected in support for limiting the role of the military in the control and
development of atomic energy, demands for immediate demobilization of troops,
and opposition to peacetime conscription. While appreciating the limits of
American military power, many citizens also recognized the important role that
anti-Nazi resistance forces and British and Soviet troops had played in the ultimate
Allied victory over the Axis powers.

In short, majority opinion in America believed in neither the omniscience nor
the omnipotence of the United States; peace and security depended on continued
American cooperation with other nations, whether major or minor powers. Finally,
most Americans demanded that the administration pursue an internationalist
foreign policy—multilaterally rather than unilaterally run. They considered economic problems the basis of threats to world peace, and felt that these could be
settled through aid and negotiation.

By 1950 a dramatic shift in this outlook had taken place, and it contributed to
the emergence of McCarthyism. It was a reaction that differed considerably from
the conservative reaction following World War I. The earlier Red Scare had been a
direct product of the passions and fears wrought by American involvement in the
war, and represented a distinct domestic political conservatism. In contrast,
McCarthyism was not directly a product of the war, since it appeared not in 1945
but in 1950, nor was its thrust overtly anti-progressive. Instead it was the product
of the Cold War confrontation between the United States and the Soviet Union and
the resulting obsession on the part of Americans with national security. Because
this confrontation was viewed not in terms of power politics but in distinctly
moralistic terms, it led to no less than an oversimplified belief in the possibility of,
indeed demand for, victory over the Soviet Anti-Christ.

This change in national opinion was in great part shaped by the rhetoric of the
Truman administration. In the period 1945-1949—that is, before Senator
McCarthy's Wheeling speech—the Truman administration conducted foreign policy
debate along narrowly anti-communist lines. To secure support for its containment
policy, from 1947 through 1949 administration rhetoric vastly oversimplified the
choices confronting the nation; it also characterized international change in terms
of crisis and national security. Indeed, the administration's anti-communist
rhetoric, the thrust of its appeals both before and after McCarthy's Wheeling
speech, did not differ substantively from that of McCarthy and his conservative
congressional supporters.

After 1945 the Truman administration had gradually, yet distinctly, renounced
the priorities of the Roosevelt administration. The bases for this shift are to be
found in two dominant strains of Truman's thought: a deep distrust of Soviet

objectives, and a belief in the importance of military superiority. In contrast to Roosevelt's sophisticated international approach, which relied on negotiation and détente, Truman's outlook—an outlook shaped by his World War I experience, his active participation in the American Legion, and his antipathy to the isolationism and anti-militarism of the 1930's—was based on the primacy of power in international politics. Although an avowed internationalist and advocate of peace, Truman believed that peace could best be secured through military deterrence and alliances. Unlike Roosevelt, whose distrust of the Soviet Union was mitigated by an expediential wartime alliance and an appreciation that Soviet involvement in Eastern Europe was as legitimate a security objective as United States involvement in Latin America, Truman felt that Soviet expansion merely confirmed the Soviet leaders' perfidy and imperialistic intentions, and thus must be averted.

Accordingly, Truman's "internationalism" assumed a unilateral form in which American national interests became the sole foundation for cooperation and peace. More importantly, in 1945, and increasingly after 1948, the administration tended to subordinate traditional diplomatic or economic options to its overriding commitment to attaining superior military power. In contrast to Roosevelt's view that disagreement, even conflict, between the United States and the Soviet Union was inevitable—and possibly even salutary, insuring a diverse world order—Truman made his administration's long-term goal the achievement of "freedom" and "democracy" for the peoples of Eastern Europe, the Soviet Union, China, and the underdeveloped world. He characterized the U.S.-Soviet conflict in moralistic terms, seeing America's role as a "mission," and redefining "appeasement" to mean the failure of the United States to confront revolutionary or disruptive change head on. A sense of American omnipotence, the belief that the United States could impose its will on the postwar world, was behind the Truman administration's rhetoric on foreign policy.

Yet this shift away from Roosevelt's foreign policy developed gradually. The 1952 priorities of the Truman administration differed radically from its 1945 priorities. This shift resulted in part from Soviet actions in Eastern Europe and the United Nations, in part from the administration's reassessment of basic foreign policy questions. What would have been politically feasible in 1945 had become politically impossible by 1952, for by then the administration, trapped in its own rhetoric, could no longer even suggest that any Soviet interest in peace or negotiation was valid.

When Harry S. Truman became President of the United States on April 12, 1945, he was faced with the immediate responsibilities of concluding the war and negotiating a settlement with the Soviet Union. Roosevelt had dominated national politics since 1932; he was the unquestioned leader of Congress and of the Democratic party, and he personified reform in the public mind. These factors, coupled with Roosevelt's personal direction of American foreign policy during the war, the nature of Truman's selection as Vice-President, and his elevation to the presidency (an unknown, uninformed former Senator acceding to the office two and half months after his inauguration as Vice-President)—all helped to heighten Truman's political difficulties in succeeding FDR.

Having been elected on the Roosevelt ticket, Truman was in principle bound by Roosevelt's earlier commitments and decisions. At best he could revise or alter the direction of policy, but he was hardly in a position to set America off on a whole new course—at least not in the early months of his presidency, when he was over-whelmed by the responsibilities of his office and the problems of his succession.

In early 1945 Truman told the American public that he would fulfill Roosevelt's intentions in foreign policy. In his first public speech after taking the oath of office, and again when first addressing a joint session of Congress, Truman spelled out his administration's objectives in essentially Rooseveltian terms: a commitment to international organization as the means to preserve peace, and an emphasis on the need for mutual understanding and continued postwar allied cooperation. Despite this common rhetoric, Truman's policy did differ from Roosevelt's in both priori-ties and methods. That is, Truman significantly qualified his reference to interna-tional cooperation and mutual understanding with the statement that real security depended on a peace based on "law" and "justice."

This reference to law and justice reflected the increased influence on policy of certain men in the State Department, the White House staff, the military, and the Cabinet. Specifically, chief among these men were James Byrnes, James Forrestal, Tom Clark, George Marshall, Dean Acheson, William Clayton, Joseph Grew, Bernard Baruch, Lucius Clay, Clark Clifford, John Snyder, William Leahy, and W. Averell Harriman. These men had played no dominant role during the war because Roosevelt shared neither their excessive Russophobia nor their military orientation, or because, in some instances, they were Truman appointees. Yet Truman, who had not been involved in forming—and lacked the requisite understanding of—Roosevelt's important foreign policy decisions, felt compelled to rely on these men for advice. Given his own feelings of inadequacy, his respect for their expertise, and his sympathy for their antipathy toward the Soviet Union, Truman's dependence on these men in itself insured a marked shift in administration policy.

The identification of security with law and justice added a new dimension to administration policy toward the Soviet occupation of Eastern Europe. To Truman, the Yalta Declaration on Liberated Europe had provided for free and democratic elections supervised equally by the United States, Great Britain, and the Soviet Union. This interpretation of the vaguely worded declaration ignored, however, both military and political realities and the "spheres of influence" agreement con-cluded in October 1944 by Churchill and Stalin and tacitly acceded to by Roosevelt in the armistice agreements with Rumania, Hungary, and Bulgaria. Most impor-tantly, Truman's interpretation overlooked the declaration's unanimous-consent provision concerning the operation of the tripartite Allied Control Commission; by permitting a Soviet veto, this provision in effect ensured that the Soviet military occupation role would be a controlling one (like what had occurred in Italy, where British-U.S. military occupation had precluded the Soviets having any role whatsoever). Moreover, in view of the Soviets' strategic interest in having "friendly" governments on her borders and her expressed commitment to prevent the reestablishment, as in 1919, of a Western *cordon sanitaire,* absolutely free elections (free, that is, of Soviet intervention or pressure) were impossible for Eastern Europe. Nor was Truman's commitment to free elections in Eastern Europe wholly consistent; Truman was willing, after all, to recognize the Argentine government and to tolerate British and French colonialism. In reality, the conflict over "free elections" and "justice" for Eastern Europe masked the administration's principal concern: the extension of Soviet influence in that area.

Although the administration held to its committment, it formally hoped to avoid a complete break with the Soviet Union. At the same time, it quelled popular fears that a provocative policy would frustrate a lasting peace. Adopting a moralistic rhetoric that stressed specific commitments and abstract principles (as opposed to more real nationalistic or strategic considerations), the administration attempted to project an altruistic, noninterventionist position. In its rhetoric it pointedly sought to capture popular suspicions about Soviet restrictions on individual liberties, and ignored the fundamental questions of whether American principles of justice necessarily had universal validity and whether their application to Eastern Europe and not Latin America or European colonial areas reflected a double standard. In effect this rhetoric served to increase popular anti-communism without substantively altering the international situation. . . .

The changed rhetoric of postwar foreign policy begat a popular obsession for achieving a total victory over communism—or, what was much the same thing in the eyes of most Americans, the Soviet Union. The failure to do so, the then current reasoning went, would directly threaten American liberties and, in addition, subvert the American mission of moral leadership in the world. Accordingly, the Truman administration's foreign policy came to be judged in terms of its effectiveness in meeting the threat of communism. Since postwar rhetoric also popularized the theme of American omnipotence, it came to be believed that an American victory was inevitable—inevitable, that is, so long as the country possessed the necessary will and resolve. The Soviet threat *per se* was not considered major; Soviet gains were thought merely the result of administration errors or inaction.

In any event, such reasoning provided the basis for the belief that both the Roosevelt and Truman administrations had "lost" China and "given" Eastern Europe to the Soviet Union. It also formed popular reactions to the Soviet Union's successful atomic bomb testing (September 1949). Despite the fact that the United States retained superiority in the stockpiling of atomic weapons, the loss of its atomic monopoly severely shocked and frightened those Americans who had come to view—not without administration prodding—this monopoly as the sole guarantee of national security. In part, this reaction explains the support, admittedly among a minority of Americans, for a preventive attack on the Soviet Union before she could develop nuclear weapons of her own. More importantly, however, Americans came to believe that the Soviets' development of an atomic bomb came about neither through Soviet science nor technology, but had simply been stolen by Soviet spies.

The result was an obsessive national fear of subversion. The real threat to America's security was now believed to come from betrayals on the part of disloyal federal employees. Nor were these employees viewed as mere reformers and radicals, as the Dies and Thomas Committees had charged, but as actual foreign agents. This was Senator McCarthy's refinement on earlier charges.

The McCarthyites' post-1950 attack on the Truman administration centered on the subversive character of former New Deal personnel, who used their important jobs to betray the national interest. Dismissing the notion that certain administration decisions had been simply errors in judgment, McCarthy and his supporters instead charged that decisions so inimical to American ideals and the national interest could only have been formulated by communists or procommunists. Recent exposures of actual espionage served only to confirm the existence of a real internal-security threat. Had not the "traitor" Alger Hiss attended the Yalta Conference and participated in the "sell-out" of China and Eastern Europe? Had not lax State Department security procedures, as in the *Amerasia* case, enabled Soviet "agents" to secure national secrets? Had not Ethel and Julius Rosenberg helped Soviet agents steal the atomic bomb? Had not Judith Coplon secured a loyalty clearance and subsequently stolen FBI classified material for the Soviet Union?

The ostensibly documented nature of the McCarthyites' charges greatly enhanced their popular acceptance. While Senator McCarthy's own estimates varied from time to time, the precision of his reference to eighty-one (not eighty or eighty-five) security risks in the State Department and his contention that he had "in his right hand" evidence documenting his accusations were supremely convincing. In reality, of course, McCarthy never did provide serious evidence of an internal-security threat, nor did he or his supporters propose any measures that might effectively combat future espionage. In the main, theirs was only a search-and-destroy operation, but one with just enough of the ring of truth to it to make it effective, given the already established popular distrust of the Truman administration.

By 1950 many Americans believed that the Truman administration's loyalty procedures were inadequate to the problem of internal subversion. This belief was not based on any solid evidence of an operating Soviet spy ring, but derived from isolated, though dramatic, incidents: the *Amerasia* case; the Canadian Royal Commission disclosure; the Alger Hiss, Julius and Ethel Rosenberg, and Judith Coplon cases. In two of these instances, the Judith Coplon and *Amerasia* cases, conviction of the accused "agents" was frustrated on the procedural grounds that the FBI had resorted to unconstitutional acts in obtaining evidence or information leading to arrests. Neither case, moreover, despite the way they were dealt with in the press, posed a serious threat to the national security.

Even though nothing even faintly resembling an extensive espionage ring had been uncovered, the impact of these two cases on the public was sensational. In part, it resulted from publicity put out by the Department of Justice, which saw in these cases an opportunity to secure legislation to strengthen its own investigatory procedures. For his part, President Truman neither counteracted the Justice Department's tactics nor fully informed the public about how limited were the threats that these cases actually posed to national security. On the contrary, his rhetoric and his actions only intensified fears of Soviet subversion. Truman claimed that traditional security methods did not adequately safeguard the nation against the communist threat. Consequently, it soon came to be believed that only the most elaborate security arrangements could save the nation. Now not only nuclear scientists but janitors and gardeners were suspect. The really insidious aspect of Truman's rhetoric about loyalty and the McCarthyites' cries of betrayal was that it encouraged a popular mania for absolute security that extended beyond the prosecution of overt acts of disloyalty to a suspicion of all potentially subversive ideas.

By 1950 the administration's announced quest for absolute security had rendered it vulnerable to attacks on its own existing loyalty procedures. The public had been educated to believe in the necessity for total security. Given these stringent demands, any subversion whatsoever came to be construed as the result only of inherent government incompetence or deliberate treason. The Truman administration had no intention of establishing an effective internal-security program, the McCarthyites charged, because it was ignorant of communist espionage methods; indeed, only a full and public investigation of the matter by Congress would result in the adoption of proper safeguards. When the administration reaffirmed in 1950 its decision of two years earlier to restrict congressional access to FBI loyalty reports, it only enabled McCarthy and other congressional conservatives to assail that decision as an attempt to cover up. . . .

Rhetorical anti-communism was central to the Truman administration's political posture from 1948 on; the standard for judging every policy proposal put forth became the degree of its anti-communist thrust. In 1948, for example, Truman asserted that no one "who believes in the destruction of our form of government" should be permitted to teach children. Similarly, he affirmed that "communists shall not work for the government and our vigilance shall be unremitting." Without clearly defining real threats—or perhaps simply because they failed to—these pronouncements implied that certain beliefs were so dangerous that any measure taken to restrict them was justified.

Certainly, this view was widely held. Since 1947 the conservatives in Congress had been seeking enactment of legislation outlawing, or at a minimum requiring registration of membership in, the Communist party. Led by Karl Mundt and Richard Nixon, this campaign was initially stymied in part by opposition from both conservatives (Robert A. Taft and J. Edgar Hoover, among them) and moderates (Thomas E. Dewey). Arguing on constitutional and pragmatic grounds, these men insisted that any legislation enacted to provide surveillance of, and to impose restrictions upon, the activities of the Communist party had at the same time to uphold the civil libertarian principles of the Constitution.

Legislative proposals brought before Congress in 1949, however, included not only Mundt's and Nixon's measure—plus a similar one introduced by Senator Homer Ferguson—but a bill originally drafted by the Department of Justice in 1947. Because this measure contained three controversial proposals—the authorization of wiretapping, registration of Communist party members, and the imposition of strict penalties for unauthorized disclosures of classified information—it had consistently been denied Budget clearance on the grounds of outraging civil liberties.[1] Despite this opposition, however, the Department of Justice had continued to lobby the measure through consultations with interested Congressmen and committee chairmen, the most enthusiastic of whom was Senator Pat McCarran (Democrat, Nevada), the chairman of the Judiciary Committee.

Before the outbreak of the Korean War, in early 1950, McCarran had pressured the President and the Democratic congressional leadership for early Senate consideration of the Justice bill. Because internal-security legislation was not then a White House priority, the administration did not honor his request. The Korean War, however, drastically changed the political context of the bill by raising doubts about the effectiveness of existing internal-security safeguards. Administration cautions on the war's possible ramifications only added to this concern. It was against this background of war and possible subversion that the McCarthyites demanded the immediate enactment of internal-security legislation. Significantly, Senator McCarran then dropped the Justice bill in favor of a more drastic measure of his own.

The McCarran bill offered the Truman administration the choice of openly opposing the enactment of all internal-security legislation or proposing on its own an alternate bill that would minimize possible abuses of individual rights. Inevitably, this choice required that the administration decide whether to allow the Communist party's activities to be restricted through surveillance. The President eventually determined to adopt a moderate course. He openly opposed the bills of Mundt and Nixon, Ferguson and Olin Johnston, and McCarran on the grounds that they transgressed civil liberties and were symptomatic of unwarranted hysteria. At the same time he proposed an alternate bill, which, while upholding the Constitution, would still protect the national security.

While stressing the gravity of the internal and external threats to national security, Truman emphasized that protection must be achieved without "unduly" limiting individual liberties. Tracing the history of the people's wariness of efforts to restrict civil liberties, Truman specifically raised the historical legacy of the Alien and Sedition Acts—presented in the 1790's ostensibly to protect national security but which effectively impinged upon individual freedoms and dissent. The lesson of the Alien and Sedition Act controversy, Truman argued, was that "extreme and arbitrary security measures strike at the very heart of our free society, and that we must be eternally vigilant against those who would undermine freedom in the name of security."

In view of the frenzied climate of American politics in 1950, Truman's legislative tactics effectively immobilized his administration's efforts to defeat the McCarran bill. By introducing a rival bill instead of seeking to defeat McCarran's, he undermined his attempt to emphasize the importance of civil libertarian considerations. Indeed, his introduction of an alternate bill only served to affirm an apparent need for more effective legislation. Moreover, Truman's emphasis on civil liberties and vague references to "undue," "excessive," "arbitrary" pressures ran counter to his administration's arguments in support of its own bill.

According to the administration, Soviet aggressive aims, as manifest specifically in the Korean War, confirmed the "clear and present danger" that communism posed to all countries. Because of this danger, the administration maintained that the American Communist party, which was simply an agent of the Soviet Union (and thus of its aggression), could constitutionally be singled out. To control the subversive activities of the party and its front organizations, the administration recommended enacting a registration and report procedure. It did not, however, specifically identify those front organizations; it only vaguely proposed that the Attorney General be empowered to list such organizations.

Attempting to secure passage of its own bill over those advanced by the McCarthyites in Congress, Truman had the Department of Justice draft a statement outlining the reasons for supporting the administration. This statement, its rhetoric reflecting administration strategy, pointed out:

> The following tactical comparison may be made between S. 2311 (the measure formally supported by the Republican congressional leadership) and the proposed substitute. The substitute presents fewer constitutional questions than does S. 2311. The substitute will do one of two things: it will obtain quickly valuable information, and, when in a few months the Supreme Court has decided the Smith Act and Loyalty Order cases, we will have more guidance on the drafting of any further legislation which may be necessary; or, if simple disclosure requirements are going to be defied by some American citizens while others are dying to repel Communist aggression, then we will find that out without going through years of legal proceedings, and the Government can act accordingly.

The Truman administration thus maintained that new legislation was needed to curb potential sabotage; yet, at the same time, it opposed the measure advocated by McCarran by noting the desirability of minimizing possibly unconstitutional procedures. This dichotomy served to undercut the administration's position; the emphasis on the gravity of the security threat contrasted sharply to arguments that the administration bill reduced constitutional objections and that further legislation could be enacted when necessary. Moreover, despite the administration's line that its bill balanced the threat to internal security with the threat to civil liberties, its main thrust had in fact always been that domestic communism posed a very real threat to national security. In his August 1950 message Truman had repeatedly referred to "this period of increasing international difficulty and danger" and had stressed the need to protect American freedoms from "internal as well as external attack."

The President was also operating on politically untenable ground when, on the one hand, he commended past administration security measures and, on the other, suggested that "new circumstances" required certain adjustments of those measures. The argument was particularly unconvincing since the Truman administration had not earlier attempted to exercise leadership to secure these "adjustments," but instead had sought to prevent the enactment of the anti-communist Mundt-Nixon bill and had not in 1948, 1949, or even the spring of 1950 pressed for the enactment of an internal-security bill drafted by the Justice Department. Truman's rhetoric in 1950, describing the security problem confronting the nation, further confounded this crisis in credibility. He thus observed that "today, we face more acutely the threat of the communist movement, international in scope, directed from a central source, and committed to the overthrow of democratic institutions througout the world." But he then warned against "unwise or excessive security measures" or "undue" restrictions on civil liberties.

These remarks reveal a striking contradiction between administration rhetoric and response. Truman seemed to want to defeat the threat of subversion and yet seemed unwilling to oppose it too strongly. If the threat to the nation *was* as acute as he suggested, and if the American Communist party *was* an agent of an international conspiratorial movement committed to overthrowing democracy, then restrictions on communist activities would be neither "unwise" nor "excessive" but absolutely essential. While internal-security legislation would necessarily violate the liberties of American Communists, such legislation would be eminently justified in view of the Communists' ultimate intent to deny those rights to every non-Communist American. And if innocent individuals suffered from the legislation, even that injustice would be justifiable in light of the larger goal of guaranteeing basic liberties to (almost) all.

Thus the administration's attempts to invoke its own vigilant prosecution of communists—citing the trial and conviction of the United States Communist party leadership under the Smith Act, and the dismissal of "disloyal" federal employees under the loyalty program—at the same time it sought to secure congressional and public support for its essentially libertarian proposal, only succeeded in increasing popular mistrust. If the administration had been as vigilant in the past as it claimed to have been, then neither a new security program was needed, nor were additional security measures required.

At all events, the administration's proposal of an alternative bill failed to prevent congressional enactment of the McCarran bill. Truman was then confronted with the necessity of either signing or vetoing this bill. He vetoed it, but his reasons for doing so again failed either to develop support sufficient for upholding the veto or to create a more tolerant, less emotion-laden political climate. Despite his references to the jeopardy to civil liberties inherent in the McCarran bill, Truman maintained a vigorous anti-communist stance in his veto message—specifically, he denied that the McCarran bill was an effective anti-communist measure:

> It has been claimed over and over again that this is an "anti-Communist" bill—a "communist control" bill. But in actual operation the bill would have results exactly the opposite of those intended.
>
> It would actually weaken our existing internal security measures and would seriously hamper the Federal Bureau of Investigation and other security agencies. . . .
>
> No consideration of expediency can justify the enactment of such a bill as this, a bill which would so greatly weaken our liberties and give aid and comfort to the enemy who would destroy us. I have, therefore, no alternative but to return the bill without my approval and I earnestly request the Congress to reconsider its action.

How could an anti-communist bill aid the communists? Truman's rationale was simply not credible. Apparently, the administration was more concerned with its image than with confronting the communist threat.

Note

1. Before submission to Congress as an executive bill, any department-proposed measure first had to secure clearance from the Bureau of the Budget that it was consistent with the program outlined by the President in his State of the Union address. The Budget Bureau not only reviewed the Justice Deparment proposal but submitted it for the consideration of other interested agencies and departments.

Chapter 7 REPUBLICANS AND THE DEFEAT OF 1948

EARL LATHAM (1907-1977) was chairman of the department of political science at Amherst College, the author of *The Group Basis of Politics* and *The Politics of Railroad Coordination, 1933-1936*, and the co-author of *The Corporation in Modern Society*. Here he interprets the tensions inherent to McCarthyism within the framework of traditional American politics. Why would conservative Democrats willingly assist Republicans to win the presidency?

In considering the appearance of the Communist "issue," great weight must be given to the presidential election of 1948, for the American political system in that year failed to provide for and facilitate a decisive change in office for which the impulse had been building for a decade. It may be fairer to say that the failure was not a failure of the system so much as it was a failure of the electorate decisively to make up its mind. If it had been able to do so, the system would have recorded the result. But whether the shortcoming was in the system or in the electorate, there was no settling decision. All of the presidential votes in the election of 1948 were negative ones—more people actually voted against Truman than voted for him;

Reprinted by permission of the publishers from pp. 394-399, 422-423 of *The Communist Controversy in Washington: From the New Deal to McCarthy* by Earl Latham, Cambridge, Mass.: Harvard University Press, Copyright 1966, by the President and Fellows of Harvard College. Footnote omitted.

more people voted against Dewey than voted for him; and more people voted against Henry Wallace and Strom Thurmond than voted for either of these candidates for the White House. There was no popular majority for President in the year 1948. The significance of this fact is heightened by the behavior of the electorate in the ten years preceding the election of 1948.

If Franklin Roosevelt had thought more of the so-called third term tradition than he did, he probably would not have run for office—at least not for the presidency—in 1940. The Republicans in their own convention and conservative elements in the Democratic party—the Garners, the Farleys, and their like—would have therefore enjoyed a kind of, not vogue, and not endorsement, but respectability, perhaps, which events were to deny them. The conservative faction in the Democratic party would have had an opportunity at least to attempt to nominate a candidate more to their liking (whether he would have won or not) and the conservative perspective might have won through in the Republican party. Roosevelt's decision to run for a third term suppressed the conservative element in the Democratic party, and moderate Republicans beat the more conservative faction in the 1940 convention as they were to do in every succeeding convention until 1964. The third term, then, and the fourth term of the war years closed the normal outlets of political expression to the conservatives, and increased their anxieties in the adulation extended to the Soviet Union. Preceding pages have already dealt with the latter of these two circumstances. The first needs further clarification.

The record of elections from 1938 to 1946 shows a rise in conservative preference. As the following figures indicate, the Democratic proportion of the two-party vote for President declined from 1936 to 1944. In 1932, the Democrats had 57.4 per cent of the two-party vote; in 1936, they had 60.2 per cent; in 1940, 53.8 per cent; and in 1944, 52.6 per cent. There is an interesting result in the 1940 elections. The Democrats received 27,476,000 in 1936 and 27,243,000 popular votes in 1940, just about holding their own. The change in percentages of 1936 and 1940 occurred because about 5 million more voters came out to vote for the Republicans and against Roosevelt in 1940, the increase moving from 16,679,000 to 22,304,000, while the Democratic vote remained about the same in the two elections.

The change in the composition of both the House and Senate in the same period reflects the same trend. The Democrats had 69 seats in the Senate in 1934; 76 in 1936; 69 in 1938; 66 in 1940; 58 in 1942; 56 in 1944; and 45 in 1946. In the House, the Democrats had 319 in 1934; 331 in 1936; 261 in 1938; 268 in 1940; 218 in 1942; 242 in 1944; and 188 in 1946. Although the Democrats did a little better in each presidential year than they had in the biennial election just preceding, there is a straight decline through 1936, 1940, and 1944, and a straight decline through 1938, 1942, and 1946. . . .

Since 1896, every President has been able to count on a second term in office except William Howard Taft and Herbert Hoover. The political budget has normally been balanced between the parties in intervals of eight or twelve years, the latter figure representing the terms of the Republican candidates Taft and Hoover as extensions of eight preceding years of Republican tenure in the White House. The change from one party to the other has occurred as a function of the accumulation of resentments and disappointed expectations. People tend to vote against rather than for, which is one of the reasons that Roosevelt in effect ran against Herbert Hoover four times. The periodicity of this swing was upset and frustrated by the third term and then the Second World War that made the fourth term inevitable. The balancing of the political budget by 1948 was long overdue and a transfer of power, normal for the pattern of half a century, was expected. Not without significance in these expectations was the record of congressional elections which for over sixty years had forecast with some reliability changes in party incumbency in the White House. The victory of the Republicans in 1946 was generally assumed to forecast victory in 1948, since similar out-party successes had forecast changes in the White House in 1930, 1918, 1910, and 1882, by the loss of one or both houses by the party represented in the White House.

Communism was not a strong issue even though the Communist Party was actually riding pretty high in 1948. Although the highest membership of the party had been reached some ten years before, the year 1948 was to be the year of the party's greatest political—certainly electoral—influence. The candidate it supported was Henry Wallace and its agency was the Progressive Party which polled a million votes. Communist elements took control of the American Labor Party in New York City early in 1948, and in January endorsed Wallace for President. Ten days later the annual convention of the Progressive Citizens of America also endorsed Wallace. The move by Communist elements to line up labor unions behind Wallace failed, however. On February 2, 1948, the executive council of the AFL denounced Wallace as the "front, spokesman, and apologist" for the Communist Party and rejected his third party bid for the presidency. Lee Pressman worked to get the CIO to endorse Wallace, failed, and then resigned as general counsel for the CIO when its executive board on February 6 refused to support Wallace and the third party ticket.

The Communist issue figured lightly in the duel between Thomas Dewey and Harold Stassen for the Republican nomination. On April 10, Dewey in Nebraska said that he thought the Communist Party ought not to be outlawed. Stassen challenged him to debate the matter and on May 17 the exchange took place by radio. Stassen had counted on a tough anti-Communist line to help him in the Oregon primary, but he lost it nevertheless.

Democrats shared the opinion of Dewey and Republican leaders that their time had come in 1948. Mention has been made of the embarrassment that Truman seemed to create among the professionals in 1946. The loss of the congressional majorities in that year confirmed the feeling that he was a drag on the ticket and that he should not be the candidate in 1948. Jake Arvey, the Democratic leader from Chicago, hoped to get Truman off the ticket in the party convention in July and many worked to give the nomination to General Dwight D. Eisenhower, including leaders of the newly formed Americans for Democratic Action. On July 15, 1948, the convention nominated Harry S. Truman, and in September Elmo Roper stopped polling the electorate because it was so obvious that Dewey would win. *Life* magazine printed a picture of Dewey on a ferry in San Francisco and referred to him as the next President.

As soon as he was nominated, however, Truman challenged the Republican party to enact the platform of the party which he thought was a piece of hypocrisy, and he called the Congress into special session to achieve this end. With a little of the sense of history he claims for himself, Mr. Truman might have been reminded of the disastrous action of Herbert Hoover when he called Congress into special session in the spring of 1929 to enact farm legislation. Instead of dealing with the matter it was convened to deal with, the Congress enacted the worst tariff in the history of this sorry legislation, the Smoot-Hawley tariff. The Republican Congress Truman called into special session, of course, did nothing about the Republican party platform. Instead, it proceeded to investigate communism. On July 30, Elizabeth Bentley testified. On July 31, she testified again, naming Lauchlin Currie and Harry Dexter White. Whittaker Chambers on August 2 named Alger Hiss, and the next day Elizabeth Bentley named Nathan Gregory Silvermaster. On August 5, Truman said that the hearings were intended to distract attention from the failure of the Congress to enact the Republican party platform, and on August 7 the special session adjourned.

Although Congress had adjourned, the genie let out of the bottle in a short session could not be put back. On August 17, Chambers and Hiss confronted each other in New York and Hiss said that he recognized his accuser. On August 20, Pressman, Witt, and Abt refused to testify about possible Communist connections. On August 30, Chambers named J. Peters, and on September 27, Hiss sued Chambers. Although the Republicans seemed to have a ready-made issue with which to attack the Democrats, the fight over the Communist issue, such as it was, was waged not by the principals but by the secondaries. The House Committee on Un-American Activities, to be sure, was in the fray, and the administration countered the committee with the Department of Justice. On September 29, spokesmen in the department accused the committee of seeking election-year publicity. On September 30, acting chairman McDowell of the committee accused the department of having drawn the indictment against the eleven Communist leaders (eventually convicted) in such a way as to ensure their acquittal. On October 1, the United States attorney for the southern district of New York asked McDowell to appear before the grand jury in New York to probe his contention. On October 8, McDowell said that he had never said what he was said to have said, and the district attorney then cancelled his request for an appearance before the grand jury.

Despite all this, it may be repeated that communism was not a very great issue in the election of 1948. It had a certain amount of verbal salience but lacked deep political impact. It was a make-weight in the scales against the administration but not the heavy balance. It was on the fringes of the contest, not at the center. It was a controversy between Dewey and Stassen and between the Department of Justice and the House Committee on Un-American Activities. It was not an issue between Truman and Dewey. The Communists were not helping the administration in the election, and there could be no confusion about the direction of their support. The main issue of the campaign was whether the Democrats had not forfeited their license to remain in office because of the accumulation of petty and great griev- ances that long tenure had fostered. Most people wanted some kind of change but they were not clear what it should be, and the election failed to produce it. All it did was to register the indecision. Instead of the change forecast, Truman was to remain in the White House for four more years.

The failure of the electorate to effect a change of government in 1948 with such opportunity as the political system might permit for the release of antiwelfarist ambitions, under conditions of some political responsibility for the outcome (which inevitably would have tempered and moderated policy), produced a political com- pression that exploded in McCarthyism. The corking of tensions laid an immediate and heavy stress on the whole governmental system—in domestic matters at least— in which the White House was to be countered and frustrated at almost every turn. First, in domestic affairs, the country was leaderless, despite Mr. Truman's famous zest for action. The celebrated Fair Deal was little more than Truman's 1949 message to a *Democratic* Congress which the Congress refused to enact. Second, effective political control over domestic public policy passed from 1600 Pennsyl- vania Avenue to Capitol Hill where it was wielded by a coalition of Republicans and southern Democrats. Since the party system had failed to deliver the responsibility for such policy to the more conservative elements in the two parties, they would take it themselves. If they could not win the White House they could control the Congress. And, as had been indicated, Congress took up the special sanction in prescriptive publicity which it could wield all by itself, and which did not depend for its justification upon any action by the President or his agencies.

There is continuity in the control of the Communist issue which Truman inad- vertently placed in the hands of Congress when he called it into special session in July 1948. Despite some changes in the composition of the committees and even in their party majorities, there is a sense in which it is true that the special session did not disband for at least six years. Although the members went home from time to time, the investigation of Communists did not cease to be the business for the Congress until the issue disappeared.

And what made the issue disappear? It was the change in the administration in 1952 which was already four years overdue, for the issue was symbolic of pressures to put the government into new hands, if only temporarily. Senator Robert A. Taft showed a certain partisan realism for which he was to be strongly castigated when he said of McCarthy's reckless attacks, "If one case doesn't work, then bring up another." By 1952, the electorate was no longer indecisive. The awaited change occurred when the Republicans took both houses of Congress and the presidency. There was no great new information for the committees to find, but some of the Republican Congressmen wanted to keep things going and even to step up the tempo. . . .

The party of General Grant, Rutherford B. Hayes, Chester Alan Arthur, William McKinley, William Howard Taft, Warren Gamaliel Harding, Calvin Coolidge, and Herbert Hoover found it difficult not only to get into the White House after 1932 but to get its candidates nominated for the presidency. Herbert Hoover was shunted to one side in 1936, Vandenberg (before his conversion to internationalist causes) was defeated by Wendell Willkie, John Bricker of Ohio lost it to Dewey in 1944, Taft lost it to Dewey in 1948 and to Eisenhower in 1952. Like the Democratic party of Cleveland, Parker, and Davis which imitated the Republicans, the Republicans between 1936 and 1964 made no frontal assault upon the programs of the New Deal but only a collateral harassment, promising to keep the social gains (although not to add to them) while administering programs more economically and efficiently. There was no restoration in 1940, as there had been in 1920, following the political adjustment of creditor claims, and the prevailing leadership in successive Republican national conventions did not seem capable of obtaining it.

The decline of the New Deal after 1936 as measured by the gradual loss of Democratic seats in the House and Senate and the shrinkage of the popular margins in the presidential elections of 1940 and 1944, presaged the expected change in 1948 which did not take place. Eager for office, disappointed by frustration, the Republican party with the help of conservative Democrats took control of the Congress in 1950, found a storm leader in McCarthy, developed the technique of prescriptive publicity as a formidable weapon of political harassment, and with an assist from the timorous and defensive leadership of the Administration managed to achieve in 1952 the victory they had been denied for two decades, which the politics of eighty years promised and, according to which, was overdue.

McCarthyism in this view of the party movements of almost a century was the agent of a fundamentalist conservatism that was prepared to yield public policy to the reformers for the relatively short periods required to satisfy grievances but which expected to recover predominance when these intervals were over. McCarthy had no social program of his own and in this respect was the perfect instrument for the realization of the social aims of those who were to benefit from his attacks, for the restoration which a third term and a war had denied. The Communist issue was the cutting edge for the attack. The Communist problem lent itself to quiet and nonsensational solutions before the late forties and after 1954. When McCarthy and the Communist issue had served their purposes, they both disappeared.

The fundamentalist conservatism that McCarthy served has been an enduring aspect of the American system since the Civil War and has not been dissipated. It believes with profound faith in free enterprise, reacts to symbols that seem to threaten it, is suspicious of welfarism and other social reform, tends to stand pat, and is moved only by exigency. The stronghold of this faith in the Republican party has been centered in the Middle and Rocky Mountain West and it has not been satisfied with the moderate conservatism of the eastern states. It regards itself as the heart and soul of the Republican party, uncorrupted by the liberalism that has softened the eastern wing, and is determined to recover the conservative spirit of the 1920's and earlier times. It is pre-New Deal in its mentality. It came to office if not to power with the help of McCarthy in the three years after 1950, and may some time surge in an effort to hold time still, and perhaps even turn it back a little.

Chapter 8 McCARTHYISM AS A BIPARTISAN DOCTRINE

For many years the most popular
biography of McCarthy was by RICHARD
ROVERE (1915-1979), a veteran observer
of Washington politics and a staff writer
for the *New Yorker*. In the following excerpt
from *Senator Joe McCarthy* he describes
the fear the Wisconsin senator inspired in
both Democrats and Republicans.

It tends now to be forgotten that McCarthy was almost as successful in immobiliz-
ing the Truman administration as he later was in demoralizing the successor government. Truman denounced McCarthy, though more frequently and more boldly
after he had left the White House than before, but he could never ignore him or
disregard his large presence on Capitol Hill. McCarthy's attacks on Truman ("The
son of a bitch ought to be impeached," he told a press conference in 1951, after
Truman's recall of General of the Army Douglas MacArthur from his Far Eastern
commands) and on the executive branch under Truman forced the administration
into a series of defensive actions that used up vast stores of time, energy, and credit
with the public. Dean Acheson, Truman's Secretary of State, spent a large part of

From *Senator Joe McCarthy*, © 1959 by Richard H. Rovere. Reprinted by permission of
Harcourt Brace Jovanovich, Inc. Pp. 12-17.

1950 and the ensuing years explaining to Elks, Moose, Women Voters, Legionnaires, Steel Workers, and the rest that he was not corrupt, that he was opposed to Communism, and that he did not hire traitors. To prove its virtue, the State Department hired John Foster Dulles and fired a number of career officers McCarthy had been attacking. When Acheson was not fending off blows before Congressional committees, he was conducting American Foreign policy, which became largely a matter of assuring allies and potential allies that McCarthy really wasn't running the show in Washington, despite contrary appearances. It was difficult. "No American official who has represented this government abroad in great affairs, not even Wilson in 1918, has ever been so gravely injured at home," Walter Lippmann wrote in 1950.

The Truman administration had to be defensive and cautious, for it knew, as the Republicans at first did not, that McCarthyism was a bipartisan doctrine. It penetrated large sections of the Democratic Party and led to much disaffection (or, better perhaps, it fed on an already burgeoning disaffection). "How do people feel about McCarthy these days?" the Republican Senator from Massachusetts, Henry Cabot Lodge, Jr., asked the Democratic Governor of Massachusetts, Paul A. Dever. "Your people don't think much of him," Dever said, "but I'm afraid mine do." The Gallup Poll once tested his strength in various occupational groups and found that he had more admirers among manual workers that in any other category–and fewest among business and professional people. If the Democratic President, from the relative safety of the White House, could be relatively free with denunciations, many other Democrats found it imprudent ever to join him. Paul Douglas, of Illinois, the possessor of the most cultivated mind in the Senate and a man whose courage and integrity would compare favorably with any other American's, went through the last Truman years and the first Eisenhower years without ever addressing himself to the problem of McCarthy. Senator John Kennedy, of Massachusetts, the author of *Profiles in Courage*, a book on political figures who had battled strong and sometimes prevailing winds of opinion and doctrine, did likewise. Maurice Tobin, Truman's Secretary of Labor, once went to a Veterans of Foreign Wars convention with an anti-McCarthy speech in his pocket; sensing a pro-McCarthy climate of opinion, he left it in his pocket and talked of other matters.

In 1952, there were many people not much enchanted by the Republican Party who favored it on the ground that if the Democrats were maintained in power, they would be forever at McCarthy's mercy. The Democrats would be driven on to further demonstrations of their anti-Communist zeal, and some of these had already been ridiculous. In 1951, for example, in the course of the Senate hearings on Far Eastern policy, Dean Acheson and his immediate predecessor, General of the Army George Catlett Marshall–both of them under savage attack by McCarthy–testified that they would never so much as *consider* the recognition of Communist China or support of its admission to the United Nations. They assured the Senate that the very idea of recognition was so abhorrent to them and to other American diplomats that it was never even *discussed* in the Department of State, which simply was not the truth. Pressed further, they made a pledge, which they were in no position to keep, that the United States would never offer recognition. Deception, stupidity, stubbornness, and a commitment in perpetuity—these were the lengths to which McCarthy and McCarthyism drove these intelligent men.

On this account, many people felt that the threat he posed could be better handled by his own party. "It is this newspaper's hope and belief that McCarthyism would disappear overnight if Eisenhower were elected," the Washington *Post* said on March 24, 1952. The hope and the belief were ill-founded. Eisenhower was elected, and within two months McCarthy was harvesting surrenders on every hand, and the *Post* was begging the administration to remember "that the voice of McCarthy is not the voice of America." To a degree, though, events did seem to justify the *Post*'s view. In 1953, for example, the administration negotiated an armistice in Korea that the Democrats would almost certainly have been unable to accept—because it would have given McCarthy additional grounds for impugning their loyalty. "I would have been crucified for that armistice," Harry Truman said.

The paralysis Harry Truman suffered, though, was as nothing compared to that which in a short time overcame President Eisenhower, who had to suffer it in silence, at least through his first two years in office. Eisenhower had been forced into a large surrender even before he was elected. He had from the start looked upon McCarthy as a cad, a gutter-snipe, and he had planned a small gesture. of defiance and dissociation. He would go into McCarthy's Wisconsin and speak a few warm and affectionate words about his old chief and patron, General Marshall, whom McCarthy had all but called a traitor. ("A man steeped in falsehood . . . who has recourse to the lie whenever it suits his convenience . . . [part of] a conspiracy so immense and an infamy so black as to dwarf any previous venture in the history of man . . . [one in whose activities can be seen] a pattern which finds his decision maintained with great stubbornness and skill, always and invariably serving the world policy of the Kremlin.") Learning of Eisenhower's plans to dispute this view of Marshall—and trembling at what they were certain was the prospect of McCarthy's fury—the party leaders in Wisconsin and half a dozen other Republican politicians pleaded with him to omit that part of his speech, which he did. (In fairness, the President did, on other occasions, stoutly defend General Marshall.) McCarthy's victory was made sweeter by the fact that he himself had played no part in gaining it. He had let it be known that Eisenhower could say whatever he pleased about Marshall and that he, McCarthy, couldn't care less. He even offered to remove himself from the Eisenhower campaign train in Wisconsin if that would make the General feel any better. But so great was the fear of him that Eisenhower gave in, even though McCarthy had magnanimously said that this would not be necessary.

In 1953, the very thought of Joe McCarthy could shiver the White House timbers and send panic through the whole executive branch. I remember once, in about the middle of that year, calling upon one of the President's assistants, a man who seemed to me then, as he does today, to be well above the average in courage and candor. I had gone in search of enlightenment on a number of things, most of them as unrelated to McCarthy as it was possible for anything to be in those days. We had a friendly enough talk and toward the end of it I brought up Topic A—and of course offered the customary assurances that I would not make use of anything he said in such a way as to embarrass him or make his life more difficult than it already was. At the mention of McCarthy, his whole manner and expression changed; though he did not move from his chair or put his palms together, he assumed, figuratively, and on his face quite literally, a supplicating mien. I have no record of the exact words he used, but I have a painfully vivid memory of them. "Don't ask me," he said. "For God's sake, please don't ask me to discuss this. Not now. I'll help you as much as I possibly can, I'll talk about anything else you want. Anything. Just don't press me on this. Don't even ask me why I don't want to talk about it. Maybe someday we can talk it all over, but not now. Accept my word that my reasons are good." I have not before or since seen a grown man in a responsible position behave in such a fashion. I had the feeling that if I had made an issue of it, I might have persuaded him to see what he could do—an exchange for my promise not again to say "McCarthy" in his presence—to get me an ambassadorship or even to declassify the recipe for the hydrogen bomb. The mere mention of the Senator from Wisconsin, the mere possibility of being compelled to discuss him, had reduced this sturdy man to jelly.

Chapter 9 PERSECUTION LEFT AND RIGHT

GEORGE F. KENNAN (b. 1904) is one of the nation's most distinguished diplomats and scholars. Since 1974 he has been Professor Emeritus at the Princeton Institute for Advanced Studies. The following, from the second volume of his highly-acclaimed memoirs, presents Kennan's assessment of the ''Reds in government'' issue and describes his involvement with the John Paton Davies, Jr. case.

The circumstances . . . of my gradual separation from government in the period from 1950 to 1953 . . . were sobering and disillusioning to some extent. . . . But the strain thus imposed was heightened by the fact that these experiences ran parallel with another set of stresses, also conducive to sobriety and disillusionment, but this time with relation not to myself personally but to the government I had now served for a quarter of a century and to the society which it represented and reflected. I refer to the occurrence of, and my own involvement with, the curious wave of political vindictiveness and mass hysteria that came soon to be known as ''McCarthyism.''

I put this term in quotation marks, because I find it a very inadequate one. What was involved here was a phenomenon that existed well before the prominent appearance of Senator Joseph McCarthy on the national scene. It outlasted his abrupt

Reprinted by permission from George F. Kennan, *Memoirs, 1950-1963* (New York: Pantheon, 1972), pp. 190-3, 200-14.

and ignominious disappearance from it. He was its creature, not its creator. It was, as I say, a wave, of sorts—a wave of feeling and reaction experienced by a great many people; and Joe McCarthy, peculiarly (if unhappily) fitted by nature for just such an adventure, rode for a short time, recklessly and giddily, on its malodorous waters, contributing at one time to their ascent, at another—to their decline. It is a pity that his name came to be given to this episode in American political life. It deserved a wider and less restrictive designation.

The penetration of the American governmental services by members or agents (conscious or otherwise) of the American Communist Party in the late 1930s was not a figment of the imagination of the hysterical right-wingers of a later decade. Stimulated and facilitated by the effects of the Depression, particularly on the younger intelligentsia, it really existed; and it assumed proportions which, while never overwhelming, were also not trivial.

Those of us who served in just those years in the American embassy at Moscow or in the Russian Division of the Department of State were very much aware of this situation—aware of it at an earlier date and much more keenly than were most of our fellow citizens. It was more readily visible to us, through the circumstances of our work, than it was to others. Our efforts to promote American interests vis-a-vis the Soviet government came into conflict at many points with the influences to which this penetration led; and our own situations were sometimes affected by it. We yielded to no one, therefore, in our feeling that this was a state of affairs which deserved correction.

It is also true that the Roosevelt administration was very slow in reacting to this situation and correcting it. Warnings that should have been heeded fell too often on deaf or incredulous ears.

The situation underwent a partial and temporary improvement in late 1939 and 1940 by virtue of the effects of the Nazi-Soviet Non-Aggression Pact, which caused many American liberals to shy off from the Soviet leadership and its American followers in the Communist Party. But when in mid-1941, we found ourselves fighting on the same side as the Soviet Union in the war against Hitler, the shock of the Non-Aggression Pact was quickly forgotten; and by the end of the war, so far as I can judge from the evidence I have seen, the penetration was quite extensive—more so, probably, than at any time in the past, particularly in the hastily recruited wartime bureaucracies, the occupational establishments in Germany and Japan, and certain departments of the government normally concerned, for the most part, with domestic affairs and unaccustomed to dealing with problems of national security.

This penetration was less important, though by no means nonexistent, in the State Department, even during wartime; and never at any time did I see reason to believe that it was of such dimensions as to lead to any extensive Communist influence on the formulation of policy. Its importance there was presumably increased, to be sure, when, in the aftermath of the war, certain of the wartime agencies went into liquidation and considerable portions of their personnel were blanketed into the department. But this situation was met at a relatively earlier point by drastic tightening of security rules and standards. And the Foreign Service itself, as distinct from the Department of State, being a disciplined career organization entry into which had been largely governed in recent years by strict competitive examination, had at no time been importantly affected by the problem of foreign penetration.

By 1947, at the time I came into the State Department, this problem, as it seemed to me then and seems to me now, was well on the way to being mastered, to the extent it ever can be. In part this was the consequence of the higher security standards. In part it may be attributed to the fact that many people who had previously considered themselves friends or followers of the Soviet leadership were given cause to hesitate and to reconsider their positions as evidence increased of the brutal and undemocratic conduct of Soviet troops and authorities throughout Eastern and Central Europe, of extensive use by the Soviet secret police of foreign Communists for espionage purposes, and of growing political conflict between the Soviet Union and the United States—conflict which meant that it was no longer possible to be a follower of Soviet leadership without placing oneself in a position of disloyal opposition to one's own government. In the fact of all these developments I gained the impression by the late 1940s that Communist penetration, whatever might have been its importance in earlier years and whatever importance it might still have had from the standpoint of military espionage, was no longer a serious problem from the standpoint of its influence on American foreign policy.

All this being the case, it was with amazement and incredulity that I took note, in the years 1948 and 1949, of the growing virulence of the attacks now being launched against the administration over just this point. Even allowing for the obvious domestic-political motivation for the exploitation of an issue that held out extensive possibilities for embarrassing the administration, it seemed to me that these attacks, vastly exaggerating as they did a waning danger and throwing discredit on a great many honorable people together with a few dishonorable ones, were not only unjustifiable but misleading and destructive. . . .

Of these various involvements (and they had to do, in one way or another with several of the most prominent cases of the time) the most extensive was my connection with the long ordeal suffered by Mr. John Paton Davies, Jr. He and I had been colleagues in Moscow from 1944 to 1946. He was then, after return to Washington, attacked in 1949 and 1950 to the Policy Planning Staff, of which I was director.

Even before coming to this position on the staff, Davies had been heavily under attack from former Ambassador to China Patrick J. Hurley and other persons close to the China Lobby, because of differences arising out of his service in China, and notably his service on the staff of General Joseph W. Stilwell, in 1942-1944. His reporting on the situation there in those years, and particularly his drawing attention to the grievous weaknesses of the Chinese Nationalist government and the improbability of its success in any prolonged further conflict with the Communists, had drawn upon him the ire of that government and its friends in the United States. Its influence in American political circles, by no means insignificant, was brought to bear against him; and he soon found himself under attack—an attack vociferously supported by Ambassador Hurley—on the strange charge of desiring the very misfortunes against which he had attempted to warn.

This charge—that Davies was pro-Chinese Communist and thus the bearer of left-wing sympathies—was simply untrue. He respected the seriousness and competence of the Chinese Communists. He warned Washington against underrating their abilities and their political prospects. But he shared nothing of the ideological doctrines which had inspired the rise of their movement.

There was, in the fact that Ambassador Hurley figured so prominently among Davies's detractors, a foretaste of the curious irony that was to bedevil the later and more tragic stages of Davies's career; for Hurley himself was already then on record as boasting, in 1945, that he was "the best friend the Chinese Communists had in Chungking" and as maintaining that these latter were devoted to principles little different from our own. He would have seemed, in the light of such statements, to be a more natural target than was Davies for just the sort of attacks the latter had to endure. But this, in the peculiar atmosphere of American political life, was largely ignored, whereas the charges advanced against Davies were eagerly seized upon by persons anxious either to find scapegoats for the miseries now being suffered by the Chinese Nationalist regime or to prove the dire extent of Communist penetration into the Roosevelt administration and the State Department.

These early attacks, however, were as nothing compared to what was now, in 1950, about to begin. And for this last, I must acknowledge a share of the blame.

Addressing ourselves, in 1948 and 1949, to the problem of how to frustrate Communist efforts at penetration and subversion of the governmental systems of Western Europe and other continents, some of us in the United States government, including myself, my friend the late Allen Dulles, later deputy director and director of the Central intelligence Agency, and certain members of our respective staffs, came to the conclusion that the government had need of some sort of facilities through which there could be conducted, from time to time as need arose, operations in the international field for which it would not be proper for any of the regular departments or agencies of the government to take responsibility, or for which the regular procedures of the government were too cumbersome. We needed, in other words, an agency for secret operations. . . .

However, one difficulty was present at the start: and this was the insistence of higher governmental circles that this undertaking be coordinated with the operations of the military establishment in the conduct of what the military had taught themselves to call "black propaganda"—a device inherited from the military operations of two world wars. . . . And for this purpose, committee meetings were held, in the usual Washington fashion.

I, having a number of other duties, could not attend all these meetings personally, and I delegated various members of my staff to deputize for me at them. One of these members, assigned—in view of his experience—to such of them as concerned Far Eastern matters, was Davies. These meetings, I should add, were all, for obvious reasons, of a top-secret classification; and it never occurred to any of us that things said or done in them would be divulged to anyone except the immediate superiors, in the departments and agencies involved, of those who took part.

In the course of this work, Davies, pressed to come up with ideas as to how certain kinds of informational material could be conveyed to the Chinese Communist intellectuals, despite the severity of the censorship in Communist China, advanced a number of ideas. Some weeks later a request came from the CIA side that he elucidate one of them. A meeting was held, on November 16, 1949, attended by two individuals, ostensibly members of the CIA—men whose names and official connection were previously unknown to us and the circumstances of whose assignment to this work have never, so far as I know, been fully clarified. Davies elaborated on the project, which was a highly imaginative if not fanciful one, expecting that the matter would be discussed at the meeting. No discussion, however, took place. The CIA men listened in silence and left, presumably to report back to their superiors. If their subsequent testimony before a congressional subcommittee is to be believed, one must conclude—and it would be the most charitable conclusion possible in the circumstances—that they had a very poor understanding of what the meeting was all about and of Davies's status in particular, and came away with a most dreadful misunderstanding of what he had been trying to say, not to mention dire suspicions of his motives.

In the normal course of things, the observations and impressions of these gentlemen would have been simply reported to their superiors, and the latter, if as puzzled and disturbed as their subordinates professed to be by what Davies was understood to have said, would have taken the matter up with the State Department at a higher level (in this instance presumably with myself) and given people in that department a chance to explain and to clarify. Had Allen Dulles then been head of CIA, I am sure this would have been done. The fact is, however, that it was not. Instead, a report was filed, if I am not mistaken, with the FBI, which report then came, in the normal course of things, to the attention of such of the congressional committees as were interested. Of these, the most interested, certainly, was the Internal Security Subcommittee of the Senate Committee on the Judiciary, the so-called McCarran (later the Jenner) Committee, a body which made itself the center for the investigation of suspected instances of Communist penetration and influence in the executive branch of the government and elsewhere. In this committee, the report of Davies's supposedly subversive proposals appears to have been pounded upon with triumphant enthusiasm, and from here on out, the fat was in the fire. Charges and denunciations were at once addressed to the State Department. The latter, presumably to protect itself, allowed Davies to be subjected to a long series of formal loyalty investigations, conducted by boards appointed in some instances by itself, in others by outside bodies. All of these without exception (there were seven or eight of them, if my memory is correct) found no reason to question Davies's loyatly and exonerated him, I believe, on all counts. But this made no difference to the Internal Security Subcommittee. On August 8 and 10, 1951, Davies was haled before those of its members who cared to be present and subjected to much hostile and suspicious interrogation. Conscious of his obligation to official security, he loyally declined to describe those details of the incident which would have laid to rest the suspicions it aroused, because he had no authority to reveal them to outside parties. The man who had denounced him was then similarly summoned and questioned; and when differences were developed, as was not unnatural, between the two sets of testimony, the Subcommittee approached the Justice Department with the request that a grand jury be summoned to determine whether Davies should not be indicted for perjury. Some two years thereafter were spent in a vain effort by the chairmen of that subcommittee and its parent body to overcome the resistance of the Justice Department to taking this action. Meanwhile, of course, there had been a great deal of publicity, controversy, anguish to Davies and his family, suspensions, transfers, and harassments of every sort; and very little of this was alleviated by the fact that he was never, so far as I am aware, found guilty on any of the numerous charges.

Finally, in the year 1954, the new Republican Secretary of State, John Foster Dulles, appointed a special "Security Hearing Board," composed of five officials of other departments and agencies of the government (their chief qualification for this task appeared to have been their common lack of any sort of experience with, or knowledge of, diplomatic work) and charged them with investigating the case all over again in the light of the new security standards of the Eisenhower administration. Davies testified before this board, being assured that he would be given an opportunity to see the unclassified portions of the transcript of the hearings before any decision was arrived at. Before he could even see the transcript, however, or give his comments on it, the board, unbeknownst to him, reported to Secretary Dulles that his further employment was "not clearly consistent with the interests of the national security."; and on November 5, 1954, Davies, having never been found guilty on any charge against his loyalty, having had nothing but excellent efficiency reports from his Foreign Service chiefs for at least a decade back into the past, and having rejected the efforts of the department to induce him to resign voluntarily, was dismissed by Mr. Dulles from the service for "lack of judgment, discretion and reliability" (the Board's words)—after which the department exerted itself for several years, though unsuccessfully in the end, to deny him the pension rights to which he would normally have been entitled.

Such, then, were the bare facts of the Davies case. My own involvement in it was not extensive, but it was also not negligible; and the matter weighed on my conscience and my thoughts for years.

The incident with CIA first came to my attention soon after its occurrence, when a journalist friend in Washington came to see me and told me, in terms that left no doubt as to the date and place of the occurrence, that Davies had endeavored to infiltrate Communists into the employ of CIA. Since it was clear that there had been an egregious and deliberate violation of security, I took the matter up with CIA. An investigation ensued. It was not difficult to establish the identity of the man who had leaked the information; his case was indefensible, and I was given to understand that he was at once dismissed.

With this, I naively supposed the episode to be closed. But this was only the beginning.

There now ensued the first round of Davies's loyalty investigations. I returned from Europe in the summer of 1951 (at my own expense) to testify on his behalf before the State Department's Loyalty Board. I testified similarly, as I recall it, when the case came before the President's Civil Service Loyalty Review Board. In both of these hearings, the CIA matter, I believe, came up; but the circumstances were such that it was impossible to give a complete clarification of what had occurred.

In the summer of 1952, when I was serving in Moscow, I received letters from Davies about the efforts of the Subcommittee to have him indicted for perjury. These letters disturbed me greatly, and for a special reason. Throughout the whole period of the loyalty investigations, against Davies and others as well, I had strongly disapproved of the manner in which the congressional and other outside charges against people in the State Department had been handled by the senior officials of the department. Instead of conducting first their own independent investigations of such charges, and then either exonerating the man or taking action against him as their own investigation might warrant, these officials simply took any charges that came to them from outside, however absurd or implausible, haled the officer before a loyalty board, and said to him, in effect: "Here is what you are charged with. Defend yourself if you can. We, the department, have nothing further to do with the matter." It was then left to the accused officer to unearth evidence, sometimes from the department's own files, to establish his innocence.

It seemed to me that this procedure represented a clear evasion of the department's own responsibility. Pride, ignorance, stress of mind, or any one of a number of other causes, might have rendered the officer unwilling or unable to defend himself, even when the facts spoke for his innocence. In this case the department, having conducted no independent administrative investigation of its own, would never have known for sure what actually occurred, or even whether justice had been done to the man in question. Yet this is the way matters were handled—in Davies's case and in others. One of the charges brought against Davies from the congressional side, for example, was plainly disprovable on the basis of evidence in the department's own files, which showed the charge to rest on a clear case of mistaken identity—it was another Davies who was involved. The department, nevertheless, instead of consulting its own files and explaining to the congressmen that the charge was baseless, solemnly charged Davies with the offense before its own loyalty board, and left it to him to have the wit to unearth the evidence that cleared him. The same was done in other cases—why? I never knew. I would have suspected pusillanimity, except that this was the last thing one could suspect in Dean Acheson. I can only conclude that he was badly advised.

For me, in any case, faced with the persecution to which Davies was now being subjected, this raised a difficult problem. It meant that I had no opportunity to come to Davies's defense in a proper, secret administrative hearing before our common superiors in the department and to clarify both my own responsibility and the motives of his conduct. And now that there was a danger of his being indicted, I knew no way of helping. I immediately drafted a letter to the Secretary of State, to make my position clear. Pointing out that I was Davies's superior at the time he performed the actions over which he was being attacked, I said that "I could not stand by and see an officer suffer injury to his career or to his status as a citizen by virtue of actions performed by him in good faith as part of his best effort to carry out duties laid upon him by myself.

"The purpose of this letter," I continued, "is to to tell you that in case this matter should have any unfortunate consequences for Davies. . . . I would not be able to feel that my own position, and my usefulness generally to the government, could remain unaffected." I suggested that the Secretary might wish to tell this to the President, as well as to the Attorney General and Senator McCarran.

None of this, however, did any good. When I came back from Moscow, the matter was still roaring along. With every attack against Davies in the press, my own conscience winced. In November 1952, *Time* magazine ran a story charging Davies with being a member of a State Department group who worked up a policy paper which misrepresented General MacArthur's advice about withdrawing our troops from Korea. The allegation was quite untrue; and I at once wrote a letter for publication in the columns of the magazine. . . .

Two weeks after the appearance of that letter, I was myself subpoenaed to appear before the McCarran Committee. (I see no reason to doubt that there was a connection.) Puzzled and angered by the use of the subpoena to bring me there (I had never failed to respond to any normal invitation to appear before a congressional body, and would as a matter of course have responded to one in this instance), I duly appeared, on the afternoon of January 13, in the small and cluttered room which the Subcommittee used for its hearings. The experience was a traumatic one. I was not told who was present in the room, nor was I informed of the identity of the man who was questioning me. I did not know, at first, as I recall it, whether my interrogator was a senator or some other individual. (He was, as it proved, one of the two attorneys for the Subcommittee, Mr. J.G. Sourwine.) Nor was I told what the subject of the hearing was, or even the reason why I had been summoned. Only gradually did it become evident to me that the affair was in connection with the Davies case. I was placed under oath; and in this condition, wholly without preparation, without counsel, without the possibility of forethought, yet vulnerable to a charge of perjury if I made the slightest slip, I endured an hour or so of cryptic and carefully prepared questioning. It included, at one point, what I could only take to be a deliberate attempt to entrap me, one of them so shameless and egregious that I could hardly believe it. (It was a matter of dates, in which point I have one of the world's worst memories; and only the presence of some real but invisible guardian angel can have saved me from falling into the apparent snare.)

I survived the ordeal. I never heard anything further from the Subcommittee. There were no formal consequences. But the experience, falling as it did in that wretched winter of puzzlement and uncertainty over the mystery of my own situation vis-a-vis the new administration, was Kafkaesque. . . . I could expect, in the circumstances, no help from the State Department; and I was obliged to recognize that I had arrived at a point where my fate, as an officer of the government, was at least partially in the hands of people for whom a record of twenty-five years of faithful and honorable service meant nothing whatsoever; where one would be given no credit for it, no consideration, and no mercy—on the contrary. And not one of one's superiors in the executive branch of the government would life a finger to help. . . .

The difficulties over the Davies case were not yet at an end. With the change in administration, the Internal Security Subcommittee came to be headed, in place of the Democratic McCarran, by Senator William Jenner. His zeal in the ferreting out of hidden Communists in the State Department appeared to be no smaller than that of his predecessor. Discovering, to his evident disappointment, that the new Deputy Attorney General (the future Secretary of State, Mr. William P. Rogers) had still not moved to the indictment of Davies for perjury, he wrote (on June 11, 1953), asking for information on the status of the case. Mr. Rogers replied (on July 6) that the Davies case, together with others inherited from the previous administration, was under review "solely by appointees of the present Attorney General" and that the review had not yet been completed. All this came to my attention when, on August 28, the magazine *U.S. News & World Report* carried the excerpts of a lengthy report by the Subcommittee entitled *Interlocking Subversion in Government Departments*, in which the Davies case figured prominently.

It was obvious from this report that the ghost was still far from being laid, and my sense of frustration was now greater than ever. I could not forget that no independent administrative investigation had ever been carried out. I had had no opportunity either to acknowledge the degree of my own responsibility or to put on record my own knowledge of the case. The State Department, now in Republican hands, was less likely than ever to make any move in Davies's defense. I therefore got in touch independently with the Attorney General's office, telling them that I had information that ought to be taken into consideration before any decision prejudicial to Davies's interests was taken, and offered to come to Washington for the purpose. The Attorney General replied, naming a deputy with whom I might discuss the matter. But efforts to arrange an appointment with the latter came to nought; and we were soon back where we started.

Several more weeks passed. Then, on December 9, 1953, the *New York Times* printed lengthy excerpts of the testimony of Davies and others before the Internal Security Subcommittee, and two days later *U.S. News & World Report* followed suit, devoting nineteen pages of its issue to what it called, in a cover headline, "The Strange Case of John P. Davies." . . .

I therefore sat down and wrote a letter to the *New York Times*, the draft of which I sent, as a courtesy, to the Department of State, with an accompanying letter to the Deputy Under Secretary. Something had to be done, I wrote in this covering letter, to correct the unclarities and misapprehensions which Davies's testimony, taken by itself, would leave. "If the department," I added, "were prepared to do this, I would be happy to remain silent; but on the assumption that the department is not contemplating such a step, I propose, as Davies's former superior, to speak out."

The reply was again discouraging. People in the department failed to understand, it was said, why I wished to "rush into print."

I wrote once more, on December 14. I respected, I said, the opinions of the senior officials of the department, but "I do not feel that I can or should permit the steady damaging of Davies's public reputation to proceed further without doing what I can to help him." As for "rushing into print":

> For more than two years I have been repeatedly on the verge of coming out publicly . . . but have been restrained each time by the hope that the government itself would take the necessary steps to protect Davies's reputation. My own fear now is that my action has been delayed too long.

The letter appeared in the *New York Times* on December 17. After recounting, along the lines described above, the nature of the CIA episode, my own relation to it, and the reasons why neither Davies nor I had ever been able to give a detailed public account of the whole story, I pointed out that the matter had been reported to the security authorities before I had been able to offer any explanations or make any clarification; and this had led, I said, to

> a seemingly endless series of charges, investigations, hearings and publicity— an ordeal which has brought acute embarrassment to Davies and his family, as well as a great sense of helplessness and concern to his friends and colleagues.

I had never, I added, had the slightest reason to doubt the honesty or integrity of his motives. . . .

With the publication of this letter, my possibilities for usefulness in the matter were exhausted. Davies was never indicted (I think that here my letter and other efforts may have done some good), but shortly after this Mr. Dulles placed in motion his own investigating procedures with the result already described. I had no influence with Mr. Dulles, and further intercession with him would have been quite useless.

If I have recounted the episode in such detail here, it is partly to illustrate the viciousness of the pressures directed against individual Foreign Service officers in the atmosphere of the time and the unsoundness of the procedures by which the leaders of the executive branch of the government reacted to these pressures, but also to make clear the bearing of such experiences on my own hesitations and vacillations with respect to the question of whether to accept passively my separation from government or to fight it and attempt to remain. I was never sure that I belonged in a government where such things could happen to one's subordinates, and where one could be so powerless to defend them from obloquy and injustice.

Chapter 10 THE TWO STAGES OF McCARTHYISM

ELLEN W. SCHRECKER (b. 1938) received her Ph.D. at Harvard University and has taught at New York University and the New School for Social Research. In this excerpt from her book *No Ivory Tower*, published in 1986, she attempts to evaluate the relationship between McCarthyism and Academia. Does she seem too harsh toward liberals? Why should professors and administrators be frightened of McCarthy and his minions?

McCarthyism was amazingly effective. It produced one of the most severe episodes of political repression the United States ever experienced. It was a peculiarly American style of repression—nonviolent and consensual. Only two people were killed; only a few hundred went to jail. Its mildness may well have contributed to its efficacy. So, too, did its structure. Here, it helps to view McCarthyism as a process rather than a movement. It took place in two stages. First, the objectionable groups and individuals were identified—during a committee hearing, for example, or an FBI investigation; then, they were punished, usually by being fired. The bifurcated nature of this process diffused responsibility and made it easier for each participant to dissociate his or her action from the larger whole. Rarely did any single institution handle both stages of McCarthyism. In most cases, it was a government agency which identified the culprits and a private employer which fired them.

We know the most about the first stage of McCarthyism, for it received the most

Reprinted by permission from Ellen W. Schrecker, *No Ivory Tower: McCarthyism and the Universities* (New York, Oxford University Press, 1986), pp. 9-10, 339-41. Footnotes omitted.

attention at the time. Yet the second stage is just as important. For without the almost automatic imposition of sanctions on the people who had been identified as politically undesirable, the whole anti-Communist crusade would have crumbled. In a sense, it was this second stage that legitimated the first. Had HUAC's targets been able to survive their encounters with the committee without losing their jobs, the committee would have lost its mandate. This did not happen. On the contrary, private employers often rushed to impose sanctions on these men and women, sometimes without waiting for the official machinery to run its course. The fate of the Hollywood Ten is illustrative here. When these radical screen-writers and directors refused to cooperate with HUAC in October, 1947, it was not clear which side had won, the witnesses or the committee. The movie studios' decision to fire the Ten before either the judiciary or public opinion had delivered a verdict may well have influenced that outcome as significantly as the Supreme Court's later refusal to review their conviction for contempt. Other employers followed the studios' example. By the time the investigative furor that characterized the first stage of McCarthyism abated in the late fifties, thousands of people had lost their jobs. And thousands more, whether realistically or not, feared similar reprisals and curtailed their political activities.

Every segment of society was involved. From General Motors, General Electric, and CBS to the *New York Times*, the New York City Board of Education, and the United Auto Workers, there were few, very few, public or private employers who did not fire the men and women who had been identified during a first-stage investigation. The academic community went along as well and dismissed those of its members McCarthy, HUAC, and the FBI had nominated for such treatment. There were quite a good number of these people, for the nation's faculties housed hundreds of men and women whom official and unofficial red-hunters were to single out as undesirable. Exact figures are hard to come by, but it may well be that almost 20 percent of the witnesses called before congressional and state investigating committees were college teachers or graduate students. Most of those academic witnesses who did not clear themselves with the committees lost their jobs. . . .

At no point did the college teachers, administrators, and trustees who cooperated with McCarthyism by evicting unfriendly witnesses and other suspected Communists from their faculties admit that they were repressing dissent. On the contrary, in their public statements and in the documentary record that they produced, they often claimed that they were standing up to McCarthyism and defending free speech and academic freedom. It is important, therefore, to go beyond the rhetoric of the period and examine what these people were doing rather than what they were saying. They said that they were opposing Senator McCarthy and the more rabid red-baiters of the period. Yet, when given an opportunity to transform that opposition into something more concrete than words, almost all of these essentially liberal academics faltered. Either they participated in and condoned the dismissals or else, when they opposed them, did so in such a limited fashion that they must have known they would not succeed. . . .

Even at the time, civil libertarians discussed the "chilling effect" of McCarthyism and noted the political reticence that blanketed the nation's colleges and universities. Marxism and its practitioners were marginalized, if not completely banished from the academy. Open criticism of the political status quo disappeared. And college students became a silent generation whose most adventurous spirits sought cultural instead of political outlets for their discontents. Their teachers, as Lazarsfeld and Thielens so devastatingly reveal in *The Academic Mind*, played it equally safe, pruning their syllabi and avoiding controversial topics. . . .

Yet, to look at the academic world's self-censorship is to explore only one aspect of the intellectual fallout of McCarthyism. We must also, and more importantly, examine the scholarship that was done. The fifties were, of course, the heyday of consensus history, modernization theory, structural functionalism, and the new criticism. Mainstream scholars celebrated the status quo, and the end of ideology dominated intellectual discourse. To what extent these developments were a response to the political repression of the day is something that demands further study. The often explicitly anti-Marxist tenor of so much of this oeuvre certainly raises questions about its relationship to the anti-Communist purges that were taking place at exactly the same time. Previous writers have either ignored the connection or else asserted, more as a matter of faith than anything else, that McCarthyism perverted the scholarship of the fifties. Certainly, it is possible that McCarthyism had a malign intellectual as well as political effect, but we cannot accept such a conclusion without evidence. We need further study of the period's main intellectual artifacts as well as serious research into what the nation's college professors thought and taught during the McCarthy years.

By the 1950s the academy had displaced all other institutions as the locus of America's intellectual life. The ideas that shaped the way Americans perceived themselves and their society developed on the nation's campuses. Most of the men and women who articulated those ideas were college teachers. They were not, however, isolated from the political repression that touched their institutions. And, in fact, many of the nation's leading intellectuals were directly involved with one or another aspect of McCarthyism. The American historian and present Librarian of Congress Daniel Boorstin named names for HUAC; Lionel Trilling, perhaps the leading literary critic of the day, chaired a Columbia committee that developed guidelines for congressional witnesses; and Talcott Parsons, whose formal paradigms shaped much of American sociology, participated in the AAUP's special survey of the Cold War academic freedom cases. How these activities affected these men's work, if at all, is certainly worth considering. . . .

McCarthyism also affected the institutional life of this nation's colleges and universities. Here, it is hard to escape the conclusion that the failure to protect academic freedom eroded the academy's moral integrity. Professors and administrators ignored the stated ideals of their calling and overrode the civil liberties of their colleagues and employees in the service of such supposedly higher values as institutional loyalty and national security. In retrospect, it is easy to accuse these people of hypocrisy, of mouthing the language of academic freedom to conceal something considerably more squalid. Opportunism and dishonesty existed, of course, but most of the men and women who participated in or condoned the firing of their controversial colleagues did so because they sincerely believed that what they were doing was in the nation's interest. Patriotism, not expedience, sustained the academic community's willingness to collaborate with McCarthyism. The intellectual independence so prized by American academics simply did not extend to the United States government.

The extraordinary facility with which the academic establishment accommodated itself to the demands of the state may well be the most significant aspect of the academy's response to McCarthyism. It was the government, not some fringe group of right-wing fanatics, which initiated the movement to eliminate Communism from American life. It administered the first stage of McCarthyism, acting through the agency of investigating committees and the FBI to identify political undesirables on campus. It let the universities handle the second stage and get rid of the targeted individuals. In another era, perhaps, the academy might not have cooperated so readily, but the 1950s was the period when the nation's colleges and universities were becoming increasingly dependent upon and responsive toward the federal government. The academic community's collaboration with McCarthyism was part of that process. It was, in many respects, just another step in the integration of American higher education into the Cold War political system.

The academy did not fight McCarthyism. It contributed to it. The dismissals, the blacklists, and above all the almost universal acceptance of the legitimacy of what the congressional committees and other official investigators were doing conferred respectability upon the most repressive elements of the anti-Communist crusade. In its collaboration with McCarthyism, the academic community behaved just like every other major institution in American life. Such a discovery is demoralizing, for the nation's colleges and universities have traditionally encouraged higher expectations. Here, if anywhere, there should have been a rational assessment of the nature of American Communism and a refusal to overreact to the demands for its eradication. Here, if anywhere, dissent should have found a sanctuary. Yet it did not.

Part Three

McCARTHYISM
AND
MASS
MOVEMENTS

Chapter 11 POPULISM GONE SOUR

PETER VIERECK (b. 1916) is a Pulitzer
Prize-winning poet and professor of history at
Mt. Holyoke College. Among his numerous
books are *Conservatism: from John Adams to
Churchill, The Unadjusted Man,* and *Meta-
politics: The Roots of the Nazi Mind.* In this
selection he argues that Populism and
McCarthyism were radically anticonservative.
What does he mean by this? How does he
define "mass man"?

During the Jacobin Revolution of 1793, in those quaint days when the lower classes
still thought of themselves as the lower classes, it was for upper-class sympathies
and for *not* reading "subversive leftist literature" that aristocrats got in trouble.

Note the reversal in America. Here the lower classes seem to be the upper
classes—they have automobiles, lace curtains and votes. Here, in consequence, it is
for alleged lower-class sympathies—for "leftist" sympathies—that the aristocrats are
purged by the lower class.

From Peter Viereck, "The Revolt Against the Elite," in Daniel Bell, ed., *The Radical Right*
(New York: Anchor Books, 1963), pp. 162-170. The Bell book selection is excerpted from
Professor Viereck's longer section on this subject in his out-of-print book *The Unadjusted Man*
(Boston: Beacon Press, 1956) and in the paperback reprint *Conservatism Revisited and the New
Conservatism* (New York: The Free Press, 1965).

In reality those lower-class sympathies are microscopic in most of that social register (Lodge, Bohlen, Acheson, Stevenson, and Harvard presidents) which McCarthy is trying to purge; even so, leftist sympathies are the pretext given for the purge. Why is it necessary to allege those lower-class sympathies as pretext? Why the pretext in the first place? Because in America the suddenly enthroned lower classes cannot prove to themselves psychologically that they are now upper-class unless they can indict for pro-proletariat subversion those whom they know in their hearts to be America's real intellectual and social aristocracy.

Ostensibly our aristocrats are being metaphorically guillotined for having signed, twenty years ago, some pinko-front petition by that egghead Voltaire (a typical reversal of the 1793 pretext) and for having said, not "Let them eat cake," but "Let them read books" (violation of loyalty oath to TV). Behind these ostensible pretexts, the aristocratic pro-proletarian conspirators are actually being guillotined for having been too exclusive socially—and, even worse, intellectually—at those fancy parties at Versailles-sur-Hudson. McCarthyism is the revenge of the noses that for twenty years of fancy parties were pressed against the outside window pane.

In Populist-Progressive days and in New Deal days, those same noses were pressed with openly radical, openly lower-class resentment. During 1953 and 1954, the same noses snorted triumphantly with right-wing Republicanism. This demagogue's spree of symbolically decapitating America's intellectual and social upper class, but doing so while shouting a two hundred per cent upper-class ideology, suggests that McCarthyism is acutally a leftist instinct behind a *self-deceptive* rightist veneer. This combination bolsters the self-esteem of sons of Democratic urban day laborers whose status rose into stuffy Republican suburbia. Their status rose thanks to the Communism-preventing social reforms of Roosevelt. Here for once is a radicalism expressing not poverty but sudden prosperity, biting the New Deal hand that fed it.

What figure represents the transition, the missing link, between the often noble, idealistic Populist-Progressives (like that truly noble idealist, La Follette) and the degeneration of that movement into something so different, so bigoted as McCarthyism? According to my hypothesis, that transition, that missing link is Father Charles Coughlin. All liberals know that Coughlin ended by defending Hitler in World War II and preaching the vilest anti-Semitism. They sometimes forget that Coughlin began his career by preaching social reforms to the left of the New Deal; his link with Populism and western Progressivism emerges from the fact that Coughlin's chief panacea was the old Populist panacea of "free silver," as a weapon against Wall Street bankers, eastern seaboard intellectuals, and internationalists, three groups hated alike by democratic Populists and by semi-fascist Coughlinites. And Coughlin's right-wing fascist anti-Semitism sounds word for word the same as the vile tirades against "Jewish international bankers" by the left-wing egalitarian Populist, Ignatius Donnelly.

On the surface, Senators like Wheeler and Nye (originally Progressives and campaigners for La Follette) seemed to reverse themselves completely when they shifted—in a shift partly similar to Coughlin's—from "liberal" Progressives to "reactionary" America Firsters. But basically they never changed at all; throughout, they remained passionately Anglo-phobe, Germanophile, isolationist, and anti-eastern-seaboard, first under leftist and then under rightist pretexts. Another example is Senator McCarran, who died in 1954. McCarran ended as a McCarthyite Democrat, hating the New Deal more than did any Republican. This same McCarran had been an eager New Dealer in 1933, voting for the Wagner Act and even for the NRA. Yet throughout these changes, he remained consistently anti-internationalist, anti-British, anti-eastern-intellectual.

Broadening the generalization, we may tentatively conclude: the entire midwest Old Guard Republican wing of today, journalistically or vulgarly referred to as "conservative," does not merit that word at all. Theirs is not the traditional conservatism of a Winston Churchill or of a Burke or of our own *Federalist* papers. Theirs is not true American conservatism in the sense in which Irving Babbitt defines indirect democracy (in his great book *Democracy and Leadership*), as opposed to plebiscitarian, Tom Painean direct democracy. "Conservative" is no proper label for western Old Guard Republicans, nor for their incongruous allies among the status-craving, increasingly prosperous, but socially insecure immigrants in South Boston and the non-elite part of the east. What all these groups are at heart is the same old isolationist, Anglophobe, Germanophile revolt of radical Populist lunatic-fringers against the eastern, educated, Anglicized elite. Only this time it is a Populism gone sour; this time it lacks the generous, idealistic, social reformist instincts which partly justified the original Populists.

Many of our intellectual aristocrats have helped to make the McCarthyite attack on themselves a success by denouncing McCarthyism as a rightist movement, a conservative movement. At first they even denounced it as a Red-baiting, anti-Communist movement, which is exactly what it wanted to be denounced as. By now they have at least caught on to the fact that it is not anti-Communist, has not trapped a single Red spy—whether at Fort Monmouth, the Voice of America, or the State Department—and is a major cause of the increased neutralism in Europe, McCarthy being the "Typhoid Mary" of anti-Americanism.

But although American liberals have now realized that McCarthyism is not anti-Communist (which is more than many American businessmen and Republicans have realized), they have still not caught on to the full and deep-rooted extent of its radical anti-conservatism. That is because they are steeped in misleading analogies with the very different context of Europe and of the European kind of fascism. Partly they still overlook the special situation in America, where the masses are more bourgeois than the bourgeoisie. I am speaking in terms of psychology, not only of economics. A lot more is involved psychologically in the American ideal of the mass man than the old economic boast (a smug and shallow boast) that simply "everybody" is "so prosperous" in America. "Every man a king" is not true of America today. Rather, every man is a king except the kings.

The real kings (the cultural elite that would rank first in any traditional hierarchy of the Hellenic-Roman West) are now becoming declassed scapegoats: the eggheads. The fact that they partly brought that fate on themselves by fumbling the Communist issue does not justify their fate, especially as the sacred civil liberties of everybody, the innocent as much as the guilty, must suffer for that retribution.

America is the country where the masses won't admit they are masses. Consequently America is the country where the thought-controllers can self-deceptively "make like" partiotic pillars of respectability instead of admitting what they are: revolutionaries of savage direct democracy (Napoleon plus Rousseau plus Tom Paine plus the Wild West frontier) against the traditional, aristocratic courts and Constitution and against the protection of minority intellectual elites by the anti-majoritarian Bill of Rights. The McCarthyites threaten liberty precisely because they are so egalitarian, ruling foreign policy by mass telegrams to the Executive Branch and by radio speeches and Gallup Poll. The spread of democratic equal rights facilitates, as Nietzsche prophesied, the equal violation of rights.

Is *liberté* incompatible with sudden *égalite*? It was, as people used to say in the Thirties, "no accident that" an American Legion meeting in New York in July, 1954, passed two resolutions side by side—the first condemning another Legion branch for racial discrimination (the "Forty and Eight" society) and the second endorsing McCarthyism. This juxtaposition is noted not in order to disparage the long overdue anti-bigotry of the first resolution. Rather, the juxtaposition is noted in order to caution the oversimplifying optimism of many liberal reformers who have been assuming that the fight for free speech and the fight for racial tolerance was synonymous.

Admittedly not all nationalist bigots have yet "caught on" to the more lucrative new trend of their own racket. Many will continue to persecute racial minorities as viciously as in the past, though surely decreasingly and with less profit. Because of the Southern atmosphere of Washington, the anti-segregation resolution could not be repeated when the Legion met there a month later.

Often untypical or tardy about new trends, the South is more opposed to the good cause of Negro rights and to the bad cause of McCarthyism than the rest of the nation. One Southerner (I am not implying that he represents the majority of the South) told me he regards as Communistic the defenders of the civil liberties of any of our several racial minorities; then he went on to reproach the North for "not fighting for its civil liberties against the fascist McCarthy."

The same day I heard that statement, I read an account of a McCarthy mass meeting in the North at which racial discrimination was denounced as un-American and in which anyone defending civil liberties against McCarthy was called Communistic. At the same meeting, a rabbi accused the opposition to Roy Cohn of anti-Semitic intolerance. Next, Cohn's was called "the American Dreyfus Case" by a representative of a student McCarthyite organization, Students for America. This young representative of both McCarthyism and racial brotherhood concluded amid loud applause: "Roy Cohn and Joe McCarthy will be redeemed when the people have taken back their government from the criminal alliance of Communists, Socialists, New Dealers, and the Eisenhower-Dewey Republicans."

This outburst of direct democracy[1] comes straight from the leftist rhetoric of the old Populists and Progressives, a rhetoric forever urging the People to take back "their" government from the conspiring Powers That Be. What else remained but for Rabbi Schultz, at a second Cohn-McCarthy dinner, to appeal to "the plain people of America" to "march on Washington" in order to save, with direct democracy, their tribune McCarthy from the big bosses of the Senate censure committee?

Bigotry's New Look is perhaps best evidenced by McCarthy's abstention, so far, from anti-Semitic and anti-Negro propaganda and, more important, by countless similar items totally unconnected with the ephemeral McCarthy. A similar juxtaposition occurs in a typical New York *Times* headline of September 4, 1954, page one: PRESIDENT SIGNS BILL TO EXECUTE PEACETIME SPIES; ALSO BOLSTERS BAN ON BIAS. Moving beyond that relatively middle-of-the-road area to the extremist fringe, note the significant change in "For America." This nationalist group is a xenophobic and isolationist revival of the old America First Committee. But instead of appeasing the open Nazis who then still ruled Germany, as in the old-fashioned and blunter days of Father Coughlin, "For America" began greatly expanding its mass base in 1954 by "quietly canvassing Jewish and Negro prospects."

And so it goes. From these multiplying examples we may tentatively generalize: Manifestations of ehtnic intolerance today tend to decrease in proportion as ideological intolerance increases. In sharp contrast, both bigotries previously used to increase together.

If sociologists require a new term for this change (as if there were not enough jargon already), then at least let it be a brief, unponderous term. I would suggest the word "transtolerance" for this curious interplay between the new tolerance and the new intolerance. Transtolerance is ready to give all minorities their glorious democratic freedom—provided they accept McCarthyism or some other mob conformism of Right or Left. I add "or Left" because liberals sometimes assume conformism is inevitably of the Right. Yet "Right" and "Left" are mere fluctuating pretexts, mere fluid surfaces for the deeper antiindividualism (antiaristocracy) of the mass man, who ten years ago was trying to thought-control our premature anti-Communists as "warmongers" and who today damns them as "Reds" and who ten years from now, in a new appeasement of Russia, may again be damning them as "Wall Street warmongers" and "disloyal internationalist bankers."

Transtolerance is the form that xenophobia takes when practiced by a "xeno." Transtolerant McCarthyism is partly a movement of recent immigrants who present themselves (not so much to the world as to themselves) as a two hundred per cent hate-the-foreigner movement. And by extension: hate "alien" ideas. Transtolerance is also a sublimated Jim Crow: against "wrong" thinkers, not "wrong" races. As such, it is a Jim Crow that can be participated in with a clear conscience by the new, non-segregated flag-waving Negro, who will be increasingly emerging from the increased egalitarian laws in housing and education. In the same way it is the Irishman's version of Mick-baiting and a strictly kosher anti-Semitism. It very sincerely champions against anti-Semites "that American Dreyfus, Roy Cohn"; simultaneously it glows with the same mob emotions that in all previous or comparable movements have been anti-Semitic.

The final surrealist culmination of this new development would be for the Ku Klux Klan to hold non-segregated lynching bees.

At the same moment when America fortunately is nearer racial equality than ever before (an exciting gain, insufficiently noted by American-baiters in Europe and India), America is moving further from liberty of opinion. "Now remember, boys, tolerance and equality," my very progressive school-ma'am in high school used to preach, "come from cooperation in some common task." If Orwell's 1984 should ever come to America, you can guess what "some common task" will turn out to be. Won't it be a "team" (as they will obviously call it) of "buddies" from "all three religions" plus the significantly increasing number of Negro McCarthyites, all "cooperating" in the "common task" of burning books on civil liberties or segregating all individuals of "all three" religions?

It required Robespierre to teach French intellectuals that *égalité* is not synonymous with *liberté*. Similarly, Joseph McCarthy is the educator of the educators; by his threat to our lawful liberties, he is educating American intellectuals out of a kind of liberalism and back to a kind of conservatism. The intellectual liberals who twenty years ago wanted to pack the Supreme Court as frustrating the will of the masses (which is exactly what it ought to frustrate) and who were quoting Charles Beard to show that the Constitution is a mere rationalization of economic loot— those same liberals today are hugging for dear life that same court and that same Constitution, including its Fifth Amendment. They are hugging those two most conservative of "outdated" institutions as their last life preservers against the McCarthyite version of what their Henry Wallaces used to call "the century of the common man."

Our right to civil liberties, our right to an unlimited nonviolent dissent, is as ruggedly conservative and traditional as Senator Flanders and the mountains of Vermont. It is a right so aristocratic that it enables one lonely individual, sustained by nine non-elected nobles in black robes, to think differently from 99.9 percent of the nation, even if a majority of "all races, creeds, and colors," in an honest democratic election, votes to suppress the thinking of that one individual.

But what will happen to that individual and his liberties if ever the 99.9 percent unite in direct democracy to substitute, as final arbiter of law, the white sheets for the black robes?

Note

1. What do we mean by "direct democracy" as contrasted with "indirect democracy?" Let us re-apply to today the conservative thesis of Madison's tenth *Federalist* paper and of Irving Babbitt's *Democracy and Leadership*.

Direct democracy (our mob tradition of Tom Paine, Jacobinism, and the Midwestern Populist parties) is government by referendum and mass petition, such as the McCarthyite Committee of Ten Million.

Indirect democracy (our semi-aristocratic and Constitutionalist tradition of Madison and the *Federalist*) likewise fulfills the will of the people but by *filtering* it through parliamentary Constitutional channels and traditional ethical restraints.

Both are ultimately majority rule, and ought to be. But direct democracy, being immediate and hotheaded, facilitates revolution, demagogy, and Robespierrian thought control, while indirect democracy, being calmed and canalized, facilitates evolution, a statemanship of *noblesse oblige*, and civil liberties.

Chapter 12 THE STATUS THEORY

In 1955 DANIEL BELL (b. 1919) edited
The New American Right, in which a
number of prominent scholars interpreted
McCarthyism as a response to a variety of
"status resentments" born of postwar
prosperity. In the following excerpt, from a
revised version of his own contribution to
the volume, Bell, professor of sociology at
Harvard University, summarizes much of
this controversial approach. How does he
characterize the "Populist temper"? What is
his definition of "Americanism"? What do
"status anxieties have to do with the
phrasing of American foreign policy
objectives in "moralistic terms"?

For Europeans, particularly, the Communist issue must be a puzzle. After all, there
is no mass Communist party in the United States such as one finds in France and
Italy; the Communist party in the U.S. never, at any single moment, had more than
100,000 members. In the last five years, when the Communist issue entered the
national scene, the Communists had already lost most of the political influence
they once had. The Communist unions had been expelled from the CIO[1]; the
Progressive party, repudiated by Henry Wallace, had fizzled; and they were fast
losing strength in the intellectual community.

It is true that liberals have tended to play down the Communist issue. And the
contradictory stand of the Truman administration compounded these confusions
and increased the alarms: on the one hand, leading members of the administration,

Reprinted with permission of The Macmillan Company from *The End of Ideology* by Daniel
Bell. ©by The Free Press, a Corporation 1960. Pp. 109-123. Most footnotes omitted.

including Truman himself, sought to minimize the degree of past Communist infiltration; on the other hand, the administration let loose a buckshot charge of security regulations which had little regard for personal liberties and rights. The invasion of South Korea and the emotional reaction against the Chinese and Russian Communists, which carried over to domestic Communists; the disclosures, particularly by Whittaker Chambers, of the infiltration of Communists into high posts in government and the existence of espionage rings; and, finally, the revelations in the Canadian spy investigations, in the Allan Nunn May trial in Britain, and in the Rosenberg case that the Soviets had stolen U.S. atom secrets, all played a role in heightening national tension.

But even after the natural effects of all these are taken into account, it is difficult to explain the unchallenged position so long held by Senator McCarthy. It still fails to take into account the extensive damage to the democratic fabric that McCarthy and others were able to cause on the Communist issue, as well as the reckless methods disproportionate to the problem: the loyalty oaths on campuses, the compulsive Americanism which saw threats to the country in the wording of a Girl Scout handbook, the violent clubbing of the Voice of America (which under the sensible leadership of anti-Communists, such as Bertram D. Wolfe, had conducted intelligent propaganda in Europe), the wild headlines and the senseless damaging of the Signal Corps radar research program at Fort Monmouth—in short, the suspicion and miasma of fear that played so large a role in American politics. Nor can conventional political analysis shed much light on him or his supporters. Calling him a demagogue explains little; the relevant questions arise in relation to whom and what he was demagogic about. McCarthy's targets were indeed strange. Huey Long, the last major demagogue, had vaguely attacked the rich and sought to "share the wealth." McCarthy's targets were intellectuals, especially Harvard men, Anglophiles, internationalists, the Army.

But these targets provide the important clues to the right-wing support, a "radical right," that backed him, and the reasons for that support. These groups constituted a strange mélange: a thin stratum of soured patricians like Archibald Roosevelt, the last surviving son of Theodore Roosevelt, whose emotional stake lay in a vanishing image of a muscular American defying a decadent Europe; the "new rich"—the automobile dealers, real estate manipulators, oil wildcatters—who needed the psychological assurance that they, like their forebears, had earned their own wealth, rather than (as in fact) through government aid, and who feared that "taxes" would rob them of that wealth; the rising middle-class strata of the various ethnic groups, especially the Irish and the Germans, who sought to prove their Americanism (the Germans particularly because of the implied taint of disloyalty during World War II); and, finally, unique in U.S. cultural history, a small group of intellectuals, some of them cankered ex-Communists, who, pivoting on McCarthy, opened up an attack on liberalism in general.

If this strange coalition, bearing the "sword of the Lord and Gideon," cannot be explained in the conventional terms that are applied to American politics, what can? One key concept is the idea of "status politics," an idea which has been used by Richard Hofstadter to deal with the status anxieties of the old aristocracy, and by S. M. Lipset with the status fears of the new rich.

The central idea of the status politics conception is that groups that are advancing in wealth and social position are often as anxious and politically feverish as groups that have become *déclassé*. Many observers have noted that those groups which have lost their social position seek more violently than ever to impose on all groups the older values of a society which they once represented. Lipset has demonstrated that groups on the rise, in order to establish themselves, may insist on a similar conformity. This rise takes place in periods of prosperity, when class or economic interest-group conflicts have lost much of their force. And Hofstadter has argued further that economic issues take on importance in American political history only during the depressions, while in periods of prosperity "status" issues emerge. But these issues, usually "patriotic" in character, are amorphous and ideological.

These political forces, by their very nature, are unstable. McCarthy himself, by the logic of his own political position, and by the nature of his personality, and to go to an extreme. And he ended, finally, by challenging Eisenhower. It was McCarthy's great gamble. And he lost, for the challenge to a Republican president by a Republican minority could only have split the party. Faced with this threat, the party rallied behind Eisenhower, and McCarthy himself was isolated. In this respect, the events prove the soundness of the thesis of Walter Lippmann and the Alsops in 1952 that only a Republican president could provide the necessary continuity of foreign and domestic policy initiated and maintained by the Fair Deal. A Democratic president might have polarized the parties and given the extreme Republican wing the license to lead the attack; the administration of a moderate Republican could act as a damper on the extreme right.

The lessening of international tensions after the settlement in Korea confirmed McCarthy's defeat. Yet McCarthy has to be understood in relation to the people behind him and the changed political temper which these groups have brought. He was the catalyst, not the explosive force. These forces still remain.

There are several consequences to the changed political temper in American life, most notably the introduction on a large scale of "moral issues" into political debate. By and large, this is new. Throughout their history, Americans have had an extraordinary talent for compromise in politics and extremism in morality.

The saving grace, so to speak, of American politics, was that all sorts of groups were tolerated, and the system of the "deal" became the pragmatic counterpart of the philosophic principle of toleration. But in matters of manners, morals, and conduct—particularly in the small towns—there has been a ferocity of blue-nose attitudes unmatched by other countries.

The sources of this moralism are varied. This has been a middle-class culture, and there is much truth to the generalization of Max Scheler, that moral indignation is a disguised form of repressed envy and a peculiar fact of middle-class psychology. In aristocratic cultures, with their free-and-easy ways, with their search for pleasure and their concentration on aestheticism, one rarely finds moral indignation an aspect of their temper. Some Catholic cultures, wordly in their wisdom and tolerant of human frailties, do not look with horror at gambling, drink, or even easy sexual conduct; disapproval is tempered with a sense of the inevitability of sin, and salvation is of the other world, not this; theft after all is a venial disgrace, but pride bears the stain of the mortal sin.

Moral indignation—and moralism—are characteristic of religions that have abandoned otherworldly preoccupations and concentrate on this worldly concerns. In Protestantism, such a displacement finds piety giving way to moralism, and theology to ethics. Becoming respectable represents "moral" advancement, and regulating conduct, i.e., being "moral" about it, has been a great concern of the Protestant churches of America.

This moralism, itself not unique to America, is linked to an evangelicism that is unique. There has long been a legend, fostered for the most part by literary people, and compounded by sociologists, that America's has been a "puritan" culture. For the sociologists this has arisen out of a mistaken identification of the Protestant ethic with the Puritan code. Puritanism and the "New England mind" have played a large intellectual role in American life. But in the habits and mores of the masses of the people, the peculiar evangelicism of Methodism and Baptism, with its high emotionalism, its fervor, enthusiasm, and excitement, its revivalism, its excesses of sinning and of high-voltage confessing, has played a much more important role. Baptism and Methodism have been the favorite American religious creeds, because they were the rustic and frontier religions. In his page on "Why Americans Manifest a Sort of Fanatical Spiritualism," Alexis de Tocqueville observed: "In all states of the Union, but especially in the half-peopled country of the Far West, itinerant preachers may be met with who hawk about the word of God from place to place. Whole families, old men, women and children, cross rough passes and untrodden wilds, coming from a great distance, to join a camp-meeting, where, in listening to these discourses, they totally forget for several days and nights the cares of business and even the most urgent wants of the body."

The Baptist and Methodist churches grew, while the more "respectable" Protestant bodies remained static, precisely because their preachers moved with the advancing frontier and reflected its spirit. "In the camp-meeting and in the political gathering logical discourse was of no avail, while the 'language of excitement' called forth an enthusiastic response," H. Richard Niebuhr has observed.

The revivalist spirit was egalitarian and anti-intellectual. It shook off the vestments and the formal liturgies and preached instead the gospel and roaring hymn. This evangelicism was reflected in the moralism of a William Jennings Bryan, a religious as well as an economic champion of the West, and in the urban revivalism of a Dwight Moody and the Y.M.C.A. movement that grew out of his gospel fervor. The evangelical chruches wanted to "improve" man, whereas the liberals wanted to reform institutions. The former were the supreme champions of prohibition legislation and Sabbath observance. *Reform in their terms meant not a belief in welfare legislation but in the redemption of those who had fallen prey to sin*—and sin meant drink, loose women, and gambling.

This moralism, so characteristic of the American temper, had a peculiar schizoid character: it would be imposed with vehemence in areas of culture and conduct—in the censorship of books, the attacks on "immoral art," etc., and in the realm of private habits; yet it rarely was heard regarding the depredations of business or the corruption of politics. On this the churches were largely silent.

The moralizing temper had another consequence: the reinforcement of the "populist" character of American society. Long ago, travelers to these shores noticed the extreme egalitarianism of American manners and customs and warned of the "leveling" consequence of the glorification of the common, rather than the uncommon, man: for if one holds that each man is as good as the next, it is easy to say, as has often been the case, that no man can claim to be better than the next. Unfortunately, good and better are never defined. That no man should claim birth alone as the inherent possessor of a status is understandable; in that respect each man is as good as the next. But populism goes further: that some are more qualified than others to assert opinions is vehemently denied.

The populist imprint on American life has had its positive as well as negative sides. The idea of the "right of the people to know" is an underpinning of the guarantees of free press, of unrestrained inquiry, and of unhampered discussion. But in a populist setting, it operates without a sense of limits and often becomes an invasion of privacy. For what is it that "the people" have a right to know? One's morals and habits? One's political views? The earlier "reformers," self-appointed guardians of morals, insisted on the right of scrutiny of private conduct in the name of public decency. Later Congressional investigators have insisted that the right to inquire is not bounded by legislative purpose but is an inherent aspect of the process of becoming the "public watchdog."

All this, in itself, would be less injurious to privacy—and freedom—if moralism and the populist conceptions of democracy were not also tied to a distinctive aspect of social control: the control of conduct, and the operation of sanctions against individuals through "public opinion" rather than law. Law, at least in the past, because it is tradition-bound and restrictive, is inhibitive of change and often has not squared with the experiences and needs of a people. But as the hard-won residue of human encounter with injustice, it sets up a strict set of procedures and a strict set of rules in admitting evidence and determining guilt. Americans, as an impatient people, however, have often been impatient with law, and the quicker sanctions of vigilantism and shaming through opinion have predominated. Moreover, the small-town character of much of the American temper derives its strength from the whispered play of gossip, from regulating conduct through public opinion rather than law. This was the exercise of conformity that was attacked so savagely by Sinclair Lewis in his *Main Street*, and the attack on the American small town was the leitmotif of the social criticism and literature of the twenties.

While in American culture the small town has been "defeated" (although in popular culture it has merged with the brassier tones of Hollywood), in American politics it has still held sway. A disproportionate percentage of the Congress, because of the gerrymandering of districts by rural-dominated legislatures, comes from small towns; these men usually have longer tenure and seniority, and the temper of the Congress, as an ideology, reflects the pseudo-egalitarian attitudes of the small town. So long as world-experiences could be assimilated into the perceptions of the small town, i.e., so long as one translated all problems into the small-town setting, the dichotomy of politics and moralism could prevail. Business was business, and the church was church; and politics was a business. But with the growth of international ideologies, the breakdown of market mechanisms, the bewildering complexities of economic decisions, the rise of submerged groups, the anxieties of decision-making became overwhelming.

American political attitudes towards China and the defeat of Chiang Kai-shek is probably the clearest case in point. As Denis Brogan has pointed out, Americans, in their extraordinary optimism, find it hard to stand defeat; it is a sickening thrust at the omnipotence which, as an unconscious self-image, underlies American power. Hence, if Chiang Kai-shek's regime came toppling down, it was easier to ascribe the reason to betrayal—by the State Department or by intellectuals—than to recognize the complex reasons involving an understanding of the breakdown of Chinese institutions since the Republic of 1911, and the failure, because of civil war and invasion, to create a viable political structure in China.

The cry of betrayal and the charge of conspiracy is an old one in American politics. One of its chief roots is in the political Populist movement, which, in its grievances against the industrial order, found its devils among those who symbolized the monetary and credit system. Populism arose, after the Civil War, among the poor farmers of the South and West. It was a protest movement against the railroads, which by freely manipulating freight rates were able to "tax" the farmer unduly, and against the bankers, who by tightening money and credit and raising the interest rates made it difficult for the farmer to buy seed or pay off mortgages. While the grievances were real, and often legitimate, what the Populists could not perceive was that a system, and not individuals, was to blame. But politics is rarely won by attacking a system. The case of Tom Watson of Georgia is one in point. Watson, who ran for vice-president on the Populist ticket in 1896, was a pioneer muckraker whose "Watson's Jeffersonian Weekly" made pungent analyses of the system of tenant land tenure, of credit manipulation, and other evils in American life. But after the turn of the century, the Populist movement became fragmented, with large chunks of it following Bryan into the Democratic party, while other elements went over to the socialists. Watson became more rancorous. He attacked Wall Street, the international bankers, and finally the Jews. The identification of Jews with money power was an old one. Ignatius Donnelley, the spokesman for Midwestern populism, had made this a central theme of his widely read novel *Caesar's Column* years earlier. Donnelley, however, had regarded the Jews as victims, since by virtue by medieval exclusions money-lending was one of the few trades open to them. Watson made the Jews the active agents of a closed conspiracy for world control. Watson was elected to the U.S. Senate, from Georgia, in 1920. He became the prototype of the new crop of Southern demagogues, Alabama's Tom Heflin, Mississippi's Theodore Bilbo, and Georgia's Eugene Talmadge. And yet, when he died, he could still be mourned by Eugene Debs as one who had fought for the people during his life.

In the twisted strands of Populism one finds other, strange tales which on the surface seem metamorphoses, but which at bottom represent the workings out of the underlying Populist temper. William Lemke and Gerald Nye came out of the vigorous North Dakota Non-Partisan League, an independent grouping of radical farmers which, finding itself unable to operate outside the two-party system, had captured the Republican party of the state. North Dakota progressivism was one of the spearheads of reform and social legislation of the twenties and thirties; public power, anti-injunction laws, regulation of child labor, etc. Nye led the famous investigation of the munitions makers during the thirties which, to the sorrow of the historian, made the overly simple identification of the causes of war coterminous with the hunger for profits of the "merchants of death."

These men were "terrible simplifiers." All politics was a conspiracy, and at the center of the web were the "international bankers" and the "money changers." Thus, when war loomed in the late thirties, the suspicion of the bankers which was the root of the crabbed Populist mentality became focused on the Jews, and one found the strange spectacle of William Lemke running for president of the United States in 1936 on a ticket organized by Father Coughlin and his Social Justice Movement. (The candidacy was supported by Dr. Franics Townsend, whose old-age scheme featured a device to increase the circulation of money, while Father Coughlin, who became a national figure because of his radio sermons in the mid-thirties, had started out as a money reformer with the nickname of "Silver Charlie.") These simplifications, now somewhat attenuated, still formed a backdrop for more recent events. But other forces were at work, too.

An unsettled society is always an anxious one, and nowhere has this been truer than in the United States. In an egalitarian society, where status is not fixed, and people are not known or immediately recognizable by birth or dress, or speech or manners, the acquisition of status becomes all-important, and the threats to one's status anxiety-provoking. Gunnar Myrdal, in his investigation of the Negro problem in America, pointed out that class antagonisms are strongest between "adjacent" classes rather than between the very bottom and the top. Thus, in the South, the deepest emotional resentment of the Negro has come from the poor whites, and particularly from those once-poor whites who, having risen, sought more than ever to emphasize their distance from those below them. As one once was more royalist than the king, one becomes more traditionalist than even the settled families, and, in the case of nationality groups, more compulsively American than the older families.

The socio-psychological attitude that Myrdal discerned in the South has been equally characteristic of the immigrant pattern in American life. As each successive wave of people came over, they grouped together and viewed the next wave with hostility and fear. In the nineteenth century, the xenophobic strain was one of the deepest currents in American life. Before the Civil War, the Catholic was the chief target. There were riots, lynchings, and the burnings of convents in Boston in the 1820's. In 1832, the anti-Catholic movement was spurred by the publication of a book, *Foreign Conspiracy Against the Liberties of the United States,* by Samuel F. B. Morse, who in the popular textbooks is accorded recognition only as a leading portrait painter and as the inventor of the telegraph. Fearing the spread of papal influences in Metternich's Europe, Morse formed the Anti-Popery Union to fight the Church. Out of its agitation grew a political party, the Native Americans, which sought to exclude all foreigners and to extend the naturalization period before citizenship to twenty years. The nativist sentiment elected James Harper mayor of New York in 1843 and was responsible for the nomination of Millard Fillmore—who had succeeded to the presidency in 1850 on the death of President Taylor—for the presidency again in 1856 on the Know—Nothing ticket. Anti-Catholic agitation was pushed into the background by the Civil War, but the tensions have remained to this day. In the East, Catholic political power came to the fore in the large urban cities of Boston, New York, Jersey City, and Chicago. In the Midwest it remained a political issue in the latter half of the nineteenth century through the agitation of the American Protective Association and the fundamentalist Protestant churches.

But what began as religious discrimination turned, in the decades that followed the Civil War, into social distinctions; these came when the rise of new social classes began to create status demarcations. In the expansion and prosperity of the 1870's and 1880's, Oscar Handlin points out, "Many a man having earned a fortune, even a modest one, thereafter found himself laboring under the burden of complex anxieties. He knew that success was by its nature evanescent. Fortunes were made only to be lost; what was earned in one generation would disappear in the next. Such a man, therefore, wished not only to retain that which he had gained; he was also eager for the social recognition that would permit him to enjoy his possessions; and he sought to extend these on in time through his family. . . . The last decades of the nineteenth century therefore witnessed a succession of attempts to set up areas of exclusiveness that would mark off the favored groups and protect them against excessive contact with outsiders. In imitation of the English model, there was an effort to create a 'high society' with its own protocol and conventions, with suitable residences in suitable districts, with distinctive clubs and media of entertainment, all of which would mark off and preserve the wealth of the fortunate families."

The process of status demarcation, associated largely with wealth in the 1890's, in more recent years has been a problem for the rising ethnic groups which have sought recognition of their new position in American life. But the older means of such distinction have disappeared, because in the mass consumption economy all groups can easily acquire the outward badges of status and erase the visible demarcations. So it is largely through politics that the rising ethnic groups began to assert their new power and social position.

These elements of moralism, populism, Americanism, and status anxieties achieved a peculiar congruence in the fifties because of the changed nature of American politics: the emergence of foreign policy as the chief problem of politics. The politics of the 1930's were almost entirely domestic, and the sharp political conflicts of that decade were around economic issues, and the divisions in interest-group terms. The debate whether or not to go to war, although sharp, was extremely brief, and the war years were characterized by a high degree of national unity. But with the postwar emergence of Soviet Russia as the dominant force on the European continent, the breakup of the old colonial empires, the eruption of Communist challenges in China and southeast Asia, and the war in Korea, the debate on the war from 1930-41, that was interrupted so abruptly by Pearl Harbor was brought back, albeit in disguised form. The attempt to pin a charge of treason on the Democrats, the new nationalism of Bricker and Knowland, the reckless actions of McCarthy, represented, in extreme, aspects of that first debate. Thus the new issues no longer represented old interest-group or internal power divisions, but the playing-out of old frustrations and anxieties.

Few "symbols" are more representative of this change than the role of Dean Acheson. In the early days of the New Deal, Acheson, a young lawyer, resigned as Assistant Secretary of the Treasury in protest against the "tinkering" with the dollar and the departure from orthodox practices; and Acheson was one of the symbols of conservative protest against the New Deal. A decade and a half later, as Truman's Secretary of State, he had become the symbol of the "radical" policies of the Fair Deal. In those terms, of course, the conceptualization was meaningless.

But the fact that the arena of politics was now foreign policy allowed the moralistic strains to come to the fore. One of the unique aspects of American politics is that, while domestic issues have been argued in hardheaded, practical terms, with a give-and-take compromise as the outcome, foreign policy has always been phrased in moralistic terms. Perhaps the very nature of our emergence as an independent country forced us to constantly adopt a moral posture in regard to the rest of the world; perhaps being distant from the real centers of interest conflict allowed us to employ pieties, rather than face realities. But since foreign policy has usually been within the frame of moral rather than pragmatic discourse, the debate in the fifties became centered in moral terms. And the singular fact about the Communist problem is that, on a scale rare in American political life, an ideological issue was equated with a moral issue and the attacks on communism were made with all the compulsive moral fervor which was possible because of the equation of communism with sin.

In itself this reflects a curious change in American life. While we gain a more relaxed attitude towards private morals, we are becoming rather more extremist in public life.

The "ideologizing" of politics gains reinforcement from another, independent tendency in American life, the emergence of what may be called the "symbolic groups." These are the inchoate entities known generally in capital letters as "Labor," "Business," the "Farmers," et al. The assumption is made that these entities have a coherent philosophy, a defined purpose, and that they represent tangible forces. This tendency derives from varied sources, but the biggest impetus has come from the changing nature of economic decision-making and the changing mode of opinion-formation in modern society. The fact that major economic decision-making has been centralized in the narrow cockpit of Washington, rather than spread over the impersonal market, leads groups like the National Association of Manufacturers, the Farm Bureau, the American Federation of Labor, etc., to speak for "Business," for "Labor," for the "Farmers." At the same time there is an increased sensitivity to "Public Opinion," heightened by the use of opinion polls in which the "Citizen" (not the specific individual with his specific interests) is asked what "Business" or "Labor" or the "Farmer" should do. In effect, these groups are often forced to assume a unique identity and a greater coherence beyond what they normally do.

Political debate, therefore, moves from specific clashes of interest, in which issues can be identified and possibly compromised, to ideologically tinged conflicts which polarize the various groups and divide the society.

The tendency to convert concrete issues into ideological problems, to invest them with moral color and high emotional charge, is to invite conflicts which can only damage a society. "A nation, divided irreconcilably on 'principle,' each party believing itself pure white and the other pitch black, cannot govern itself," wrote Walter Lippmann many years ago.

It has been one of the glories of the United States that politics has always been a pragmatic give-and-take rather than a series of wars-to-the-death. One ultimately comes to admire the "practical politics" of Theodore Roosevelt and his scorn for the intransigents, like Godkin and Villard, who, refusing to yield to expediency, could never put through their reforms. Politics, as Edmund Wilson has described T. R.'s attitude, "is a matter of adapting oneself to all sorts of people and situations, a game in which one may score but only by accepting the rules and recognizing one's opponents, rather than a moral crusade in which one's stainless standard must mow the enemy down."

Democratic politics means bargaining between legitimate groups and the search for consensus. This is so because the historic contribution of liberalism was to separate law from morality. The thought that the two should be separate often comes as a shock. In the older Catholic societies ruled by the doctrine of "two swords." The state was the secular arm of the Church, and enforced in civil life the moral decrees of the Church. This was possible in political theory, if not in practice, because the society was homogeneous, and everyone accepted the same religious values. But the religious wars that followed the Reformation proved that a plural society could only survive if it respected the principles of toleration. No group, be it Catholic or Protestant, could use the State to impose its moral conceptions on all the people. As the party of the *politiques* put it, the "civil society must not perish for conscience's sake."

These theoretical foundations of modern liberal society were completed by Kant, who, separating legality and morality, defined the former as the "rules of the game," so to speak; law dealt with procedural, not substantive, issues. The latter were primary matters of conscience, with which the State could not interfere.

This distinction has been at the root of the American democracy. For Madison, factions (or divergence of interests), being rooted in liberty, were inevitable, and the function of the Republic was to protect the causes of faction, i.e., liberty and the "diversity in the faculties of men," for "freemen, 'diverse' men, fallible, heterogeneous, heterodox. opinionated, quarrelsome man was the raw material of faction."

Since faction was inevitable, one could only deal with its effects, and not smother its causes. One way, of course, was, as adopted in the federal system, to separate the powers of government, so that no faction could easily secure a monopoly of power. But Madison knew that this was not enough. The threat to liberty would be reduced by representative government, and in this *extensive republic*, as he put it, the larger number of interests would "lessen the insecurity of private rights." But representative government, as John Stuart Mill cogently pointed out, must mean the representation of all interests, "since the interest of the excluded is always in danger of being overlooked." And being overlooked, as Calhoun added, constitutes a threat to civil order.

But representative government is important for the deeper reason that by including all representative interests one can keep alive "the antagonism of influences which is the only real security for continued progress." It is the only way of securing the "concurrent majorities," which, as Calhoun argued, was the solid basis for providing a check on the tyrannical "popular" majority. For only through representative government can one achieve consensus—and conciliation.

This is not to say that the Communist "interest is a legitimate one, akin to the interest of other groups in the society, or that the Communist issue was completely irrelevant. As a conspiracy, rather than a legitimate dissenting group, the Communist movement remains a threat to democratic society. And by the criteria of "clear and present danger" democratic society may at times have to act against that conspiracy. But these are questions to be handled by law. The tendency to use the Communist issue as a political club against other parties or groups, or the tendency to convert questions of law into issues of morality (and thus shift the source of sanctions from the courts and legitimate authority to private individuals) can only create strains in a liberal society.

In the 170 years since its founding, American democracy has been rent only once by civil war. We have learnt since then, not without strain, to include the "excluded interests," the workers and the small farmers. These have secured a legitimate place in the American political equilibrium. And the ideological conflicts that almost threatened to disrupt the society, in the early years of the New Deal, have been mitigated.

The new divisions, created by the status anxieties of new middle-class groups, pose a new threat. The rancors of McCarthyism were one of its ugly excesses.

Note

1. By 1952, at the height of McCarthyism, the Communists controlled unions with fewer than five per cent of U.S. labor membership as against a peak control of unions with twenty per cent of union membership in 1944.

Chapter 13 PLURALISTS AND AGRARIAN RADICALISM

MICHAEL PAUL ROGIN (b. 1937) is a
professor of political science at the
University of California, Berkeley. His *The
Intellectuals and McCarthy: The Radical
Specter* won the American Historical
Association's Albert J. Beveridge Award for
1967. Here he sharply contradicts the views
of Viereck and Bell, interpreting
McCarthyism neither as a radical
movement nor as a cause that drew its
strength from mass support.

When McCarthy first became prominent, most liberals interpreted the danger he
posed in fairly straightforward terms. To them McCarthy was simply the most
successful of a number of conservative Republicans capitalizing on the Communist
threat to attack the New Deal at home and the Fair Deal abroad. "McCarthyism"
was a synonym for smear attacks on liberals, its roots were in traditional right-wing
politics, and its principal targets were innocent individuals and liberal political
goals. Liberals hardly minimized McCarthy's political importance, although they
had little difficulty explaining either his roots or the danger he posed.

But to many writers such traditional analysis failed to account for McCarthy's
strength. In their eyes, McCarthy was getting support not from the established

Reprinted from *The Intellectuals and McCarthy: The Radical Specter* by Michael Paul Rogin by
permission of The M.I.T. Press, Cambridge, Massachusetts. Copyright © 1967 by The Massachusetts Institute of Technology. Pp. 2-7, 261-268. Most footnotes omitted.

groups with which traditional conservatism had been associated but rather from the dispossessed and discontented. One had to wonder about any inevitable association between popular discontent and support for progressive movements of economic reform. Moreover, McCarthy continually appealed to the mass of people for direct support over the heads of their elected leaders. And the established eastern elite, unsympathetic to the Wisconsin senator, was one of his important targets. All this suggested that popular democracy constituted a real threat to the making of responsible political decisions. McCarthy appeared not in the guise of a conservative smearing innocent liberals but in the guise of a democrat assaulting the political fabric.

If faith in democracy suffered from the McCarthy period, sympathy for radicalism hardly fared better. Both the more orthodox liberal analysis of McCarthysim and those with the newer view recognized that McCarthy dominated America while traditional radical movements lay dormant. To the old-fashioned liberals, McCarthyism symbolized the death of radical protest in America. In the newer view, McCarthy was the bearer of the historical radical mission—challenging, like earlier radicals, the established institutions of American society. The McCarthy years thus ushered in a new fear of radicalism among growing numbers of intellectuals. One can date from the McCarthy period the rise of such terms as "radical Right" to go with radical Left, and left-wing "fundamentalism" to coincide with right-wing extremism.

In this new view, McCarthyism was a movement of the radical Left. For traditional liberals, the New Deal and contemporary liberalism had grown out of the protest of the pre-Roosevelt years. The newer view produced a very different history. Left-wing protest movements, democratic in their appeal to the popular masses, radical in the discontent they mobilized, had borne fruit in McCarthyism. To some, McCarthy was directly descended from an alliance between traditional conservatism and agrarian radicalism.

The term agrarian radicalism refers to the movements of rural protest that flourished between the end of the Civil War and the New Deal epoch—the Grangers, the Greenbacks, the Farmers' Alliances, the Populists, the progressives, and the Non-Partisan League. Not all these movements were exclusively rural. Progressivism in particular had an important urban wing, although it is well to remember that in state and national politics progressives most continually triumphed in rural areas.

Aside from being predominantly rural, pre-New Deal protest movements had important geographic sources of continuity. Outside the South, these movements flourished along the settled frontier. From the 1880's to the 1930's, left-wing protest politics were strongest in the West and the western Middle West. Populism outside the South received most of its support from the plains states and those bordering on them. The Non-Partisan League of 1916 to 1924 had been strongest there too. Pre-and post-World War I progressivism tended to be strong in the Middle West and weak in the East.

Agrarian radicalism thus flourished in the states of the trans-Mississippi West. Political leaders in these states were most vociferous in their support of McCarthy and supplied him with most of his votes against the senatorial censure resolution of 1954. In particular, senators from states that had supported the Populist presidential candidate in 1892 or La Follette for President in 1924 disproportionately voted against the McCarthy censure.[1]

Certainly the geographic coincidence of support for McCarthyism and agrarian radicalism can be exaggerated. The South opposed both La Follette and McCarthy, but party loyalty was more crucial than ideological commitment. Since the Populist revolt, agrarian radicalism was not strong in the eastern Middle West; but this area produced strong Republican support for McCarthy. The trans-Mississippi West, however, supported both McCarthyism and agrarian radicalism. A look at the map thus provides concrete evidence linking McCarthy to agrarian radicalism. The interpretation of McCarthy as radical democrat appears persuasive. The new view of politics implied by that interpretation seems supported by the evidence.

The present study challenges the notion that McCarthy had agrarian radical roots. Examination of the empirical evidence finds no correlation between support for agrarian radicals and support for McCarthy; consideration of the reform tradition uncovers no unique reform appeals on which McCarthy capitalized. Investigations of the McCarthy movement discloses no agrarian radical flavor but rather a traditional conservative heritage. Analysis of the new social theory questions its relevance to American history....

[The new social theory] has gained wide currency in the intellectual world, receiving the support of such prominent and thoughtful writers as Richard Hofstadter, Seymour Martin Lipset, Talcott Parsons, Edward Shils, David Riesman, Nathan Glazer, Oscar Handlin, Peter Viereck, Will Herberg, Daniel Bell, William Kornhauser. Before they wrote, McCarthyism meant something like character assassination, and Populism was the name of a particular historical movement for social reform at the end of the nineteenth century. Through their influence Populism has become an example of and a general term for anomic movements of mass protest against existing institutions—the type of movement typified by McCarthyism.

Those connecting it with the earlier movements see McCarthyism, first, as a democratic revolt of dispossessed groups against the educated, eastern elite. Like McCarthyism, agrarian radicalism is also said to have substituted moralistic, irrational appeals for a rational politics. For many writers, these movements embody a nativist mystique which, glorifying the ordinary folk, threatens the civilized restraints of a complex society.

For these writers, both movements "rejected the traditional cultural and educational leadership of the enlightened upper and upper-middle classes." Populism and La Follette progressivism identified the will of the people with justice and morality. Holding a plebiscitarian view of democracy, agrarian radicals placed the popular will above the autonomy of institutions and the desires of the various strata in the society. Since political leaders cannot function in an atmosphere of plebiscites and exposures, agrarian radicalism crippled responsible political leadership and endangered privacy. In this sense, "McCarthy is the heir of La Follette." McCarthyism and agrarian radicalism exhibit "the tendency to convert issues into ideologies, to invest them with moral color and high emotional charge which invites conflict which can only damage a society." "Beneath the sane economic demands of the Populists of 1880-1890 seethed a mania of xenophobia, Jew-baiting, intellectual baiting, and thought-controlling lynch spirit." McCarthyism is the "same old isolationist, Anglophobe, Germanophile revolt of radical Populist lunatic fringers against the eastern educated, Anglicized elite." "McCarthyism appealed to the same social groups as did 'left-wing' Populism."

Clearly such charges rest on a particular view of politics—one involving suspicion of the people, fear of radicalism, friendliness to established institutions, re-examination of the American past. The fear of mass democracy and radical protest that grew in the McCarthy years eventuated in theories of mass society and pluralism. Much of the effort to connect McCarthyism and agrarian radicalism transcends its particular historical significance and becomes relevant to general questions of social change and democratic politics. . . .

Pluralist interpretations of McCarthyism and agrarian radicalism suffer from four misconceptions. First, the pluralists see a continuity in support that does not exist and misunderstand the evolution of American politics. Second, they exaggerate the "mass" character of the agrarian radical movements. Third, they minimize the importance of the specific issues with which McCarthy and the agrarian radicals sought to deal. And fourth, they fail to understand the role of moralism in the American political tradition.

The difference in electoral support between McCarthyism and agrarian radicalism is easiest to demonstrate objectively. Both McCarthy and the agrarian radical movements did receive their strongest electoral support in rural states. Within those states, however, the groups upon which they drew were very different. Populism based itself on Scandinavian areas. Germans and Catholics tended to oppose these movements. But Germans were the chief ethnic group in McCarthy's electoral base, while significant numbers of Democratic Catholics were won over by his appeals. Where an agrarian radical supported McCarthy, as in North Dakota, this was because of a German support unusual for peacetime agrarian radicalism.

The lack of continuity in social support means that much of McCarthy's constituency had opposed agrarian radicalism. If the agrarian radical movements had the same concerns as McCarthyism, why were McCarthy's supporters not disproportionately agrarian radical? That so much of McCarthy's support came from traditional conservative constituencies suggests that many of McCarthy's underlying concerns were those that had traditionally activated the opposition to agrarian radicalism.

At the same time, the electoral evidence gives little comfort to those who have seen direct continuity from Populism or progressivism to modern liberalism and anti-McCarthyism. Where agrarian radicalism had an economic base among the poor and where it maintained a cohesive following over the years, its supporters tended to become part of the modern Democratic constituency. This placed them in opposition to McCarthy. Bob La Follette, Jr.'s 1940 Senate vote was correlated -7 with McCarthy's Senate vote twelve years later. But where agrarian radical movements rose and fell without continuity, they made little disproportionate contribution either to the modern Democratic vote or to the opposition to McCarthy.

Moreover, holding the party vote constant there was a tendency for rural areas disproportionately to support McCarthy. Many of these rural counties in South Dakota and Wisconsin, had earlier been progressive. The amount of support for McCarthy contributed by these former progressive counties was small; but pluralists could argue that it symbolizes the core of common concerns uniting McCarthyism and agrarian radicalism.

There is little question that farmers no longer dominate the Left in American politics as they did in the days of Jefferson, Jackson, and the Populists. Agrarian radicalism virtually disappeared in the decade of the New Deal and World War II. Class politics replaced sectional politics, and workers replaced farmers as the mass bulwark of the Left.

As the number of farmers declined drastically, as agriculture became more of a business on stable foundations, and as World War II and the cold war ushered in an unprecedented agricultural prosperity, the base for agrarian radicalism declined. The farmers that remained had little enthusiasm for movements of economic protest. As the larger society became more bureaucratized, as the strange forces of big labor and big government arose in the urban world, as a cosmopolitan outlook encroached on rural values, the program of agrarian radicalism seemed unable to solve the problems that continued to agitate rural society. Finally, the increased importance of foreign policy and the Communist menace brought to a head the rural concern with moral questions. The trans-Mississippi West became the center of ideological conservatism instead of agrarian radicalism.

But simply because a group plays a different role in one period of history than another is no reason to read back its later conservative politics into the earlier radical period. Marx, writing about French farmers, distinguished the role they played at the time of the first Napoleon with their role at the time of the second, fifty years later. One can make an analogous interpretation of the role of America's rural inhabitants. Not to make such distinctions is to ignore the importance of history.

The pluralists justify their ahistorical view of rural politics because they detect a moralistic thread running through its progressive and conservative phase. Populism, progressivism, and McCarthyism were all in the pluralist view mass moralistic protests against industrialization.

The first difficulty with this view arises when the "mass" character of the movements is examined. A close look at the "mass" nature of McCarthyism and agrarian radicalism suggests the gulf that separates these phenomena rather than the bonds that unite them. The difference between McCarthyism and agrarian radicalism at the grass roots is striking. McCarthy mobilized little specific organizational support outside the grass roots Republican Party organizations. He encountered little opposition from local elites. He gave little evidence of exerting a mass appeal that uprooted voters from their traditional loyalties. Agrarian radical movements, on the other hand, held hundreds of meetings, organized at the grass roots for innumerable electoral compaigns, and created new voting patterns that often influenced events after the movements themselves had disappeared. Although these mass movements had a salutary effect on American politics, they exhibited many of the effects of mass activity that the pluralists fear. McCarthyism exhibited few of these effects. It neither split apart existing coalitions nor created an organized, active mass following. If Populism was a mass movement in the sense of its grass roots appeal and McCarthyism was not, McCarthyism had "mass" characteristics, such as contempt for the rule of law and generalized hostility to cosmopolitan values, that were lacking in agrarian radicalism. But such anomic characteristics were found more among political leaders and local elites than among masses. Since McCarthyism cannot be explained by the "mass" preoccupations of the masses, one must examine the support for McCarthy among certain elite groups and the tolerance or fear of him among others. The pluralists' preoccupation with mass movements as threats to a stable, democratic group life prevents them from analyzing McCarthyism in this fashion.

When the relevant political issues are closely examined, the anti-industrial character of McCarthyism and agrarian radicalism—and therefore the alleged connection between them—also evaporates.

Like the agrarian protest movements, McCarthy drew sustenance from concrete political issues; but his issues were not the agrarian radical issues. Populism, La Follette progressivism, and the Non-Partisan League attacked industrial capitalists, not industrialization. They proposed concrete and practical economic reforms. McCarthy focused on the political not the economic order. While many McCarthy activists were in rebellion against modern industrial society, this society included—and was in their eyes dominated by—New Deal reforms of the type agrarian radicals had favored. This was a very different society from that of the "trusts" and the "robber barons" at the turn of the twentieth century, against which agrarian radicals directed their fire. Moreover, most of McCarthy's supporters on public opinion polls cared more about communism, Korea, and the cold war than they did about modern industrial society. McCarthyism could not have flourished in the absence of these foreign policy concerns.

If no direct links are sustained by the evidence, the pluralists may still retreat to the general argument that McCarthy utilized a peculiarly moralistic, agrarian radical, political style. They point to an alleged agrarian radical tendency to seek moral solutions to practical problems. As Hofstadter explains, "We are forever restlessly pitting ourselves against (the evils of life), demanding changes, improvements, remedies, but not often with sufficient sense of the limits that the human condition will in the end insistently impose upon us." The pluralists argue that as the agrarian radical world of moral certainty disappeared, this progressive optimism became frustrated. Former agrarian radicals sought scapegoats to explain their defeats. It was an easy step, for example, from the progressive belief that only special interests stood in the way of reforms to the McCarthy certainty that only treason could explain the failures of American foreign policy.

Consider, as evidence for this interpretation, the career of Tom Watson. Watson, the leading southern Populist of the 1890's, supported the political organization and economic demands of the southern Negro farmer. He made a reasoned analysis of the causes of rural misery and opposed economic panaceas. But out of frustration generated by the defeat of Populism, Watson became an anti-Negro, anti-Catholic, anti-Semitic, southern demagogue. For the pluralists, Watson's career symbolizes the development of McCarthyism. Hofstadter writes, "While its special association with agrarian reforms has now become attenuated, I believe that Populist thinking has survived in our own time, partly as an undercurrent of provincial resentments, popular and 'democratic' rebelliousness and suspiciousness, and nativism."

But here the pluralists substitute the sin of noncomparative analysis for the sin of static analysis. Examination of the moralistic character of American politics discloses that (a) prior to the New Deal political moralism was by no means confined to agrarian radicals; (b) American political moralism asserts the reality of a public interest and denies the need for basic irreconcilable conflict, and thus much of the moralistic flavor of American politics is a condition of pragmatism rather than an alternative to it; (c) McCarthy's particular moralistic preoccupations were typical of traditional conservatism more than of left-wing progressivism.

The Populist traditon could produce antidemocratic and even neofascist figures, but given the nature of American society and the absence of strong elite backing for these figures, they had little success in national politics. Tom Watson, who combined anti-Semitism with sympathy for the Soviet Union, was clearly a product of Populism gone sour; McCarthy was not.

McCarthy and the agrarian radicals came from two contrasting political traditions. Both traditions stressed self-help, but the Populists did not attack bureaucracies indiscriminately. Agrarian radicals sought to meet the threat of private bureaucracies by increasing the role of the state. The agrarian radical traditon was anti-Wall Street, anti-vested interests, anti-industrial capitalist. This tradition has been dying out as the role of left-wing protest politics has passed to the cities. Its evolution has produced Tom Watsons and Burton Wheelers, but sophisticated, humanitarian liberals like Quentin Burdick and George McGovern have been equally prominent. Perhaps their independence from Johnson on the Vietnamese war owes something to the agrarian radical heritage. McCarthy's ideological conservative tradition was anti-intellectual, antistatist, antibureaucratic, and antiforeign. Locally prestigious and wealthy elites have dominated this politics, generally attracting widespread popular support as well. McCarthy, the son of a poor farmer, was marginally outside this conservative tradition. He effectively exploited this marginality, but without the support of the conservative tradition he would have made little impact.

Behind the pluralist misinterpretation of McCarthyism and fear of agrarian radicalism lies a legitimate suspicion of mass movements. But this fear, fed by the triumph of totalitarianism in Russia, Italy, and Germany, obscures the differences among mass movements. To find radical roots for McCarthy's support is to underestimate the middle-class diversity of the American populace. For the pluralists, McCarthyism and agrarian radicalism were united by their *petit bourgeois* character. But in America the *petit bourgeois* class is both enormous and diverse. Different political movements can call on support from different segments of that class; their support can be *petit bourgeois* without being significantly related. It is a mistake to identify mass movements with authoritarianism and pressure groups with democracy. Rather there are authoritarian and democratic mass movements, just as there are authoritarian and democratic pressure groups. The Populist mass movement operated within the established constitutional framework of the republic; it was not a threat to democracy.

The danger of McCarthyism, on the other hand, while real, was not the danger of a mass movement. McCarthy had powerful group and elite support. He did not mobilize the masses at the polls or break through existing group cleavages. McCarthy's power was sustained only in part by the vague discontents of frustrated groups. Communism and the Korean War played crucial roles. The real danger posed by McCarthy should not distort our understanding of agrarian radical movements in America, nor should the pluralist criticisms of mass movements blind us to the real nature of McCarthyism.

Note

1. In 1892, Populist presidential candidate Weaver received more than 37 percent of the vote in eight states. All provided at least one vote for McCarthy on the censure resolution. (The only other state in which Weaver received as much as 25 percent of the vote was Alabama.) Cf. John D. Hicks, *The Populist Revolt* (Omaha, Neb.,: University of Nebraska Press, 1961), p. 263.

The coincidence of support for La Follette and McCarthy goes beyond the fact that both were from Wisconsin. In the censure vote, McCarthy got the support of two Republican senators in only five states—Indiana, Idaho, North Dakota, Nevada, and California. In all but Indiana, La Follette had gotten more than 30 percent of the vote in 1923; his national average (by states) was 17 percent. The one Republican senator in seven other states voted against the McCarthy censure. La Follette had exceeded his national average in all seven. Including Wisconsin, McCarthy got support on the censure resolution from twenty states. Fourteen of the eighteen states that gave La Follette more than 17 percent were among those twenty. Cf. Herbert Parzen, "A Comparative Study of the Progressive Presidential Campaigns of 1912 and 1924," unpublished Master's thesis, Department of Political Science, Columbia University, 1926, pp. 1-7; "McCarthy's Strength Centered in West, Midwest," *Congressional Quarterly* (December 3, 1954), p. 1409. No Democrats voted against the censure.

Chapter 14   AN INSTRUMENT RATHER THAN CREATOR

SEYMOUR MARTIN LIPSET (b. 1922) is
one of the nation's most important
sociologists and the author of several books
on the nature of American politics.
Currently he is professor of government
and social relations and a senior fellow at
the Hoover Institute. In 1955 he
contributed to *The New American Right*
and proposed a "status" explanation for
McCarthyism. How different is this
selection from Daniel Bell's? EARL RAAB
(b. 1919) is a widely recognized authority
on the field of intergroup relations and
executive director of the San Francisco
Jewish Community Relations Council.

McCarthyism was not a political movement. It never had members, organized chap-
ters, offered candidates, or formulated a platform. It was a tendency of the times,
which McCarthy epitomized, to which he lent his name, but of which in a way he
was finally an instrument rather than creator. He was, it is true, a particularly
suitable and capable instrument.

As a Catholic, McCarthy was able to embody the traditional anti-Communism
and the growing conservatism of that population, without the disability of Father
Coughlin's collar. And as a Wisconsinite who followed a La Follette to the Senate,
he was able to embrace the agrarian, isolationist, and ethnic sentiments of the
Midwest. In fact, the states which were the backbone of agrarian radicalism before

From pp. 220-224, 235-240, *The Politics of Unreason* by Seymour Martin Lipset and Earl
Raab. Copyright © 1970 by Anti-Defamation League of B'nai B'rith. Reprinted by permission
of Harper & Row, Publishers. Footnotes omitted.

the New Deal gave McCarthy most of his support. A direct line has often been drawn between the La Follette Progressive populist tradition and McCarthy. This line has been given different implications, however. There is little question but that McCarthy drew on the same anti-interventionist sentiment that La Follette had invoked. There is also a certain similarity between their tactics. [According to Michael Paul Rogin:]

> Both Wisconsin Senators conveyed a similar image of embattled insurgency. . . . McCarthy adopted the stance of continual attack that characterized the elder La Follette. McCarthy was a "fighter" for the people's interests, and the condemnation of respectable society only served to strengthen the image of McCarthy as "Battling Joe" just as it had worked for "Fighting Bob."

But there is more implied in the comparison than tactics. In stating that "McCarthy is the heir of La Follette," {Edward A.] Shils asks:

> What was populism if not the distrust of the effete East and its agents in the urban Middle West? Was not populism the forerunner of "grass-roots" democracy? Did it not seek to subject the government to the people's will, to tumble the mighty from their high seats, to turn legislators into registrants of the people's will? Was it not suspicious of the upper classes of the East? . . . . Did not populism allege to protect the people and their government from conspiracies, from cells of conspirators, who, contrary to the people's will and through the complacency or collusion of their rulers, were enabled to gain control of society?

Whether McCarthy personally "owed" these proclivities to the La Follette tradition is somewhat immaterial. McCarthyism did not, although the tendency prospered as a result of the consonance. Conspiracy theories in America have always leaned heavily on the concept of direct democracy, as an antidote to the secret elite who allegedly were contravening the people's will. One of the intrinsic links between conspiracy theory and monism is the anti-constitutional bias of direct democracy. This is one of the rationales for by-passing the rules, as McCarthy and McCarthyism often did. When McCarthy's censure was being formally considered by the Senate, Herman Walker said "the ninety-six senators are not the judges. The 150,000,000 Americans are the judges of the trial of McCarthy."

Likewise, conspiracy theories, by their nature, are anti-intellectual and invariably focus on some overeducated secret elite. In this case, the most singular link with midwestern populism was the identification of that elite with the eastern Brahmins. Even that identification coincided with the predispositions of other supporting populations: the Irish Catholics, the small businessmen, the new Texas millionaires.

As a matter of fact, McCarthy's was as abstract and "clean" an approach to conspiracy theory as any in American history and may have partly fallen of its own weight as a result. Since the first vague image of the Illuminati conspiracy in the eighteenth century, which also fell of its own weight, the effective conspiracy theories in America have involved two dimensions: a mysterious cabal and some less mysterious, more visible target group associated with the cabal. The offending Catholic immigrants in tandem with the papist plots served this purpose; so did alien Jewish merchants in tandem with the Elders of Zion. Even nonethnic "eastern Bankers" could serve some purpose of group visibility for the agrarian mind. McCarthy invoked none of these. His traitors were pure: leaders who had sold out to a foreign power on an individual basis. There was the standard anti-intellectual, anti-elite appeal of denigrating the Ivy League character of many of the alleged conspirators—but finally there was no cogent group identity.

On first reading, McCarthy's plot theory seemed to be stated as vehemently and as explicitly as it had ever been stated. Our deplorable situation he ascribed to "an infamy so black and a conspiracy so immense as to dwarf any previous such venture in the history of man." He seemed to accuse the President, General Marshall, many State Department officials and government leaders of being part of the plot; but after the fierce rhetoric, he invariably ended up accusing them of being failures rather than plotters. "We were not [ever before] misled and enfeebled by abstractions such as collective security and by the tortured twisted reasoning of men of little minds and less morals who for the first time in the history of this nation argue that we should not vigorously fight back when attacked."

Of course, the Senator's stock in trade and his most effective tactic was promising to "name names." In his 1950 Wheeling, West Virginia, speech which abruptly launched his anti-Communist career he said, "I have here in my hand a list. . . ." He held many such lists in his hand during his public career. Not many names were ever actually revealed. But in any case they were only, finally, names of individuals who had presumably sold out to the foreign enemy.

For McCarthyism, the enemy was an ideology, Communism. True, there was a headquarters in Moscow, but the ideology was the enemy. When General MacArthur said in 1951 that the threat to America was not from the outside but "from the insidious forces working from within which have already so drastically altered the character of our free institutions, . . ." the altered institutions themselves were his target, the "insidious forces" remaining abstract. When Senator William Jenner said that the "collectivist machine" operating in the White House, the State Department, and elsewhere "emanated from some control tower we cannot see," he illustrated the ambiguity of this approach to conspiracy. If the Kremlin was the control tower, the threat was, in one sense, external rather than internal and not really a conspiracy, but a kind of dirty war. But if the threat was that the American people were being seduced by collectivism and internationalism, thus permitting the traitors to more easily deliver us, the prime danger was in fact an ideology and not a band of conspiratorial handmaidens.

It was in this sense that McCarthy's enemy, and that of many of his cohorts, was Communism itself rather than any singular group of conspirators. McCarthy's approach to politics, in the monistic mode, was apolitical; that is, highly moralistic. But his moralism was in tune with the universalist religious framework of America and indeed with the new moral tempo of America. McCarthy was cited by friends as being "a good Catholic, but not the kiss-the-book light-the-candle Catholic."

Richard Rovere noted that "where other politicians would seek to conceal a weakness for liquor or wenching or gambling, McCarthy tended to exploit, even to exaggerate, these wayward tastes. He was glad to have everyone believe that he was a drinker of heroic attainments, a passionate lover of horseflesh, a Clausewitz of the poker table, and a man to whom everything presentable in skirts was catnip." But he could accuse President Eisenhower of dealing with "the apostles of hell," of planning to make "territorial concessions to Red China."

One biographer quotes McCarthy as saying in a home-town speech: "There are two fundamental truths of religion: there is a God who is eternal, and each and every one of you has a soul which is immortal." McCarthy then indicated that his anti-Communist crusade was not just political, and the biographer comments: "The implication was clear: the campaign was religious. God and Joe, with the voters' help, would emerge victorious."

McCarthy himself stated it clearly: "The great difference between our western Christian world and the atheistic communist world is not political . . . it is moral." The thrust was to establish anti-Communism as the religion of America, with Communism as the anti-religion. It cut across sectarian lines and blended with the secularized faith of America, although the fundamentalists could relate to it with their own more particularistic language.

Communism was being used as the broad general reference by which to identify the body of bad intentions and bad character in the world. It was not really that Communism was evil because it was atheistic, but rather that it was deemed "atheistic" because it was evil. The heart of the American religion was, simply, opposition to evil as it cohered in Communism, just as the heart of bedrock fundamentalism was opposition to evil as it cohered in Satan. Americanism was the set of values which embodied such an American religion.

In this sense, McCarthyist anti-Communism represented the ultimate movement to abstract and anomic nativism. The group identity was one of moral superiority. This had always been a characteristic of nativism, often as a kind of "cultural baggage" to strong and specific ethnic and regional ties. The appeal to ethnic and regional ties was still a subsurface nativist presence in many aspects of McCarthyism, but in general its nativism was more diffuse. On the other side of the nativist coin, it was not aliens but alien ideas which needed exorcising. Coughlin had moved toward such an abstract nativism; but in fusing his nativism with conspiracy theory, he had located a specific body of people as nativist backlash targets. In McCarthyism the same moral fervor and absolutism were present. The equating of Communism with anti-God was not new. But the relative absence of a singular cohesive body of plotters and fellow travelers was new to conspiracy theory.

Indeed, McCarthyism was more conspiracy style than conspiracy theory, more technique than theory of any kind. The technique, which bears his name, consisted of seeming to charge people with treason, without actually doing so. This involved "guilt by association," a phrase which resounded through the early 1950's in America; or innuendo; or the waving of undisclosed "lists." It spoke of conspiracy, but all it spelled out was treason and ideological defection. McCarthyism never succeeded in corporealizing the American conspiracy.

Smelser's step-by-step analysis of the development of a political movement suggests that without the designation of a specific cause for the social strain in question, there is no movement, only hysteria. He defines a hysterical belief as "a belief empowering an ambiguous element in the environment with a generalized power to threaten or destroy." He cites certain institutionalized hysterical beliefs as superstitions, fears of witchcraft, demons, spirits, and the like. A corporealized conspiracy can provide specific cause. But McCarthy's Communism as an internal threat remained generalized, and McCarthyism remained more a hysteria than a political movement.

As a hysteria, however, it was potent; and even with a "faulted" conspiracy theory, it unlocked the monistic impulses of America. Partly, McCarthy and his associates were able to do this because there were traitors, there were spies, there were some significantly placed Communist cells in America. One of McCarthy's most severe journalistic critics affirmed that "a number, even if a relatively small number, of the shots called by McCarthy in his changing lists . . . of alleged loyalty, security and 'morals' risks were later proved to be on the target." Some individuals in the clear service of a foreign power were exposed. The slavish devotion to Soviet foreign policy on the part of a few influential people was established. These people were security threats and it can be presumed that they created a great deal of mischief. But the accumulation of all their activities could not explain the plight of America, internally or on the world scene.

At that point, the hysteria took over. Throughout the country, there was a witch hunt, not so much for conspirators as for ideological defectors. The basic monistic formula was applied: Communism was evil, and those who trafficked in such evil were illegitimate and to be excluded from the market place of ideas—and even from the market place of jobs. Since ideological defection, as distinct from membership in any specific group, was a matter of varying judgment, it was pluralism which was under attack. In Washington, McCarthy conducted a lengthy and public investigation of the personnel of the Voice of America, which resulted in the discovery of no Communists, but the discharge or resignation of some thirty employees. "Black lists" of suspect personnel were established for the information of industry's hiring offices. Libraries around the country were under pressure, to which they did or did not give in, to remove arbitrarily suspect books and magazines from their shelves. For example, on one list of books, which the city manager of San Antonio said in

1953 should be burned, were "Einstein's *Theory of Relativity,* Thomas Mann's *Joseph in Egypt* and *The Magic Mountain,* . . . Norbert Wiener's *Cybernetics*; also various anthologies of poetry and folk songs, also books on sculpture, the mentally ill, alcoholics, child care, architecture and mystery novels.". . . .

McCarthyism's Failure

McCarthy's *mariage de convenance* failed to create a political movement, however, and finally proved to have had little substance. Several factors seem to have been involved: (1) the absence of a program to engage the "mass man"; (2) the absence of a corporealized target; (3) the withdrawal of conservative party support.

McCarthy ended his career bitterly attacking the Republican party and its President. But the Republican administration had already abandoned him. He had performed his best function for them in identifying Communism with the Democratic party. His continued inquiries into the loyalties of government and armed forces agencies and personnel began to be considerably less helpful to the Republican party after it had assumed the stewardship of the government. A number of Republicans, including President Eisenhower, had been only tolerant of McCarthy, embarrassed by his excesses, but this toleration had become less needful and more costly. And the economic conservatives made the belated discovery that McCarthy was not a conservative after all. When he voted, he was as likely as not to vote for more public housing, more social security, more federal subsidies. But the main point was that his single-issue usefulness, that of diverting popular votes to the Republican party in the name of anti-Communism, had been reduced.

In 1950, when McCarthy began his crusade, the Republicans were still suffering from their unexpected defeat by Truman in 1948, and the future looked grim for their party. In 1952 the party swept back into power with Eisenhower, but McCarthy did not change his anti-elitist course. He took on both Eisenhower's State Department and Army. Spurred by the treatment—or lack of preferential treatment—of an aide, David Schine, who had been drafted, McCarthy escalated an investigation of the Army into a major and decisive boomerang. Beginning an investigation of security measures at Fort Monmouth, he proceeded to publicly "discover" that the promotion of an Army dentist was an index to Communist infiltration of the Armed Services. In pursuance of this discovery, he publicly humiliated a General and demeaned the Secretary of the Army. The midwestern branch of the Republican party was still with him, but the eastern "establishment" wing of the Grand Old Party was now quite ready to abandon him as surely as it had elevated him. Vice-President Nixon, as part of the Republican establishment, maneuvered a head-on confrontation between the Army, which charged that McCarthy had used his position to get preferential treatment for his aid, and McCarthy, who claimed that the Army was just trying to impede an investigation. The hearing ran for thirty-five days on television, and as many as 20,000,000 Americans watched it at any given time. At the end of the hearing, the Senate appointed a Select Committee to investigate McCarthy's behavior on several counts, and as a result of that investigation, the Senate voted 67 to 22 to "condemn" McCarthy.

The Republican Senators divided evenly in the vote, with almost all of those from eastern states plus Michigan voting against McCarthy, while most of the members from the Midwest and far western states voted for him. The cleavage, in part, reflected the isolationist and China-oriented section of the party on one side and the internationalist wing on the other. From another perspective, it located the Senators with the closest ties to big business against McCarthy, and those coming from areas in which the party was influenced by less powerful business groups on his side.

The establishment Republicans had clearly lined up against him. McCarthy's chief armament had always been the fear to oppose him, especially on the part of public officials. These officials had the sense that while McCarthy had no organized movement, he had a strong following in the populace—a feeling which the polls corroborated. They had no confidence that there was an effective defense against his arbitrary accusations. When Eisenhower was campaigning in Wisconsin in 1952, he deliberately omitted friendly references to his old chief General Marshall, whom McCarthy had been violently attacking, lest McCarthy be offended. But, in a modern version of the tale of the Emperor's Clothes, when the Army-McCarthy hearings and the subsequent Senate action revealed that McCarthy had finally been deliberately confronted and faced down by the establishment (he was even barred from White House social events), the magical fear evaporated. It evaporated the more surely because the fight seemed to go out of McCarthy as a person after this series of events. He died three years later at the age of forty-eight without much further political ado.

But the turnabout of the conservative political party which had used an extremist instrument in classic fashion could not account for such a swift collapse of McCarthyism. And the fact that McCarthy developed no organizational apparatus to carry on his crusade was more than a personal quirk. The indication is that McCarthy had less of a political hold on the populace than he was credited with. It is not that he did not have a vast influence on the public, or that he did not continue to have a large measure of their support. Even after the Senate condemnation, 40 per cent of those with opinions supported him in the polls. But the principle of *selective support* applied, and in this case the nature of the selectivity was limited to a single issue. At a time in 1953 when about half the American people said they "supported" or "approved" McCarthy in the opinion polls, only 5 per cent indicated in a Roper poll that they would vote for him for President on a "third party" ticket against Eisenhower and Stevenson. In the spring of 1954, a poll taken by the *Boston Post* reported that 40.5 per cent of Maine voters backed McCarthy, while 41.4 per cent were against him. The same poll, however, found that only 10.6 per cent of those interviewed were in favor of Robert L. Jones, a strong supporter of McCarthy's, who was running in the Maine Republican primary against Senator Margaret Chase Smith, a bitter public opponent of the Wisconsin Senator. The vast majority, 85.5 per cent, were for Senator Smith, and she was an easy victor in the primary. Clearly, many who approved the Senator for his anti-Communist activities were not prepared to back him or candidates he favored in elections.

The greatest support for McCarthy recorded by the polls occurred when questions were phrased in terms of whether the respondents believed that McCarthy's allegations about Communists in government were true, or whether they approved of his efforts to eliminate Communists. But questions implying a more direct evaluation of the Senator himself—for example, how McCarthy's endorsement of a candidate would affect one's vote—produced a very different pattern of response. When attitude toward the existence of Communists in government was not involved, somewhere between 10 and 20 per cent were favorable, while about 30 to 40 per cent were opposed to him. Once in existence as a concept, McCarthyism became a much more salient issue to the liberal enemies of the Senator than to his conservative or militantly anti-Communist friends. The Communist issue apart, many more people reacted negatively to the mention of his name than positively. Consequently it would appear that McCarthy's support for a candidate was likely to mobilize more opposition than backing for him. According to the electoral analyst Louis Bean, in "all states where McCarthy pinpointed his charges against Democratic Senatorial candidates the Democratic candidate ran ahead of the general ticket."

McCarthy's inability to develop a committed following points up the limitations of anti-Communism as an issue. There has always been opposition to Communism on the part of the vast majority of American people. But, as Stouffer pointed out, the opinion surveys on the question have almost invariably indicated that "the internal threat of Communism has not been a matter of salient concern" among most of these people. For some, particularly the uneducated, Communism did not have to be especially salient in order to accept McCarthyism as a means of combating it. However, their acceptance of McCarthyism did not mean that they had a prime allegiance to him as a political leader.

Even in the New Deal period, survey data indicated that the bulk of the population supported the outlawing of the Communist party and approved of the original House Committee on Un-American Activities, led by Martin Dies. In November 1937, 54 per cent of a national Gallup sample favored a law permitting the police to "padlock places printing Communist literature"; only 35 per cent opposed such a measure. In June 1938, 53 per cent of a national sample indicated they were against allowing Communists to hold meetings in their community, while only 35 per cent were willing to give Communists this right. In November 1939, 68 per cent were opposed to allowing "leaders of the Communist Party [to] make speeches to student groups," and only 24 per cent approved. In June of 1942, at a time when the Soviet Union was a military ally of the United States, 50 per cent favored a law outlawing membership in the Communist party, while 36 per cent were against the proposed act. A number of surveys that inquired in 1938 and 1939 whether respondents approved of continuing the Dies Committee reported approximately three-quarters in favor.

Popular awareness of the international Communist threat undoubtedly increased in the late 1940's and early 1950's, with the advent of the Berlin blockade in 1948, the fall of China in 1949, and the outbreak of the Korean War in 1950, but public acceptance of civil liberties for Communists neither increased nor decreased. However, this never meant that anti-Communism was the most salient political issue for the majority of the American people. They were just against Communism, and to the extent that their commitment to and understanding of pluralism was dim, they saw nothing wrong with repressing radicalism even beyond Constitutional limits.

McCarthy's anti-Communism, McCarthyism, became more pertinent than usual for a large number of people not just because of McCarthy's personal demagogic talents but because he struck a nerve that was more than anti-Communist. His anti-Communism was a banner around which various segments of the population could marshal their preservatist discontents and their generalized uneasiness.

There can be little doubt that American apprehension about the Communist threat was enhanced by political events, specifically the Korean War, which began in 1950 and ended in 1954, the span of McCarthyism. But McCarthy rarely discussed the military threat posed by Communist expansionism. Rather he argued in 1952: "There is only one real issue for the farmer, the laborer, and the businessman—the issue of Communism in government." And he disparaged American intervention in Korea, saying in 1951, "So the administration which would not fight Communism at home undertook to prove to the American people that it was willing to fight Communism abroad."

McCarthy's main targets were never the North Korean or Chinese or Russian Communists—not even seriously, Communist spies in America—but rather the American establishment. This was the general target which so many Americans savored. From all evidence in the opinion polls, a sizable minority of them would have continued to use him as a way to voice their various preservatist sentiments, even after the Korean War ended; but there is no indication that they would have gone out of the way to make him their over-all political leader. The single issue was not enough; he had no political program to offer the mass populace—either the urban workers or the farmers. Leroy Gore, a Wisconsin weekly newspaper editor who had been an avid McCarthy supporter, explained his weakness in his home state by saying: "Few Wisconsin farmers have ever seen a Communist. Joe's Commie search is purely academic. . . . The price of milk isn't academic."

While it was chiefly a bread-and-butter political program that McCarthy lacked, from a technical point of view his conspiracy theory was also faulty. The enemy was an ideology; and the closest McCarthy came to personifying a group as that enemy in America was his attack on the elite. Thus, in his Wheeling speech he said:

The reason we find ourselves in a position of impotency is not because our only potential enemy has sent men to invade our shores, but rather because of the traitorous actions of those who have been treated so well by this nation. It is not the less fortunate, or members of minority groups who have been selling this nation out, but rather those who have had all the benefits the wealthiest nation on earth has had to offer—the finest homes, the finest college educations, and the finest jobs in the government that we can give. This is glaringly true in the State Department. There the bright young men who are born with silver spoons in their mouth are the ones who have been worst.

The attack on the elite recurred frequently in the writings of the extreme right. *The Freeman* magazine wrote that "Asian coolies and Harvard professors are the people . . . most susceptible to Red propaganda." In discussing McCarthy's enemies, *The Freeman* stated; "He possesses, it seems, a sort of animal, negative-pole magnetism which repels alumni of Harvard, Princeton, and Yale. And we think we know what it is: *This young man is constitutionally incapable of deference to social status.*"

This was anti-elitism, which would have an obvious appeal to the midwesterners and to the eastern urbanites of non-Anglo-Saxon extraction. Here was a prosperity-born equivalent for the economic radicalism of depressions. For the resentment created by prosperity is basically not against the economic power of Wall Street bankers or Yankees, but against their status power. Peter Viereck called this "the revenge of the noses that for 20 years of fancy parties were pressed against the outside window pane."

However, the "elite" in this case was a blurred population group. At times, the attack was just a form of anti-intellectualism. McCarthy referred to the "twisted thinking intellectual" who had taken over the State Department. When the *Facts Form* attacked the "enemy," it referred to "the socially pedigreed, the culturally acceptable, the certified gentlemen and scholars of the day, *dripping with college degrees.* . . . "And this anti-elitism was also a kind of Anglophobia, itself a variant of isolationist sentiment in America.

But while there was a heavy emphasis on the individuals, traitors, and defectors being drawn from the Ivy League elite, they were finally *individual* traitors and defectors. This experiment of building a conspiracy theory without an ethnically (or economically) identifiable group did not seem to be successful. A singular difference between McCarthy and earlier extreme right-wing anti-Communists was his lack of interest in investigating or publicizing the activities of men who belonged to minority ethnic groups. For several decades the monistic impulse in America had concentrated on Jews as the group target of anti-Communism. But McCarthy did not; to the contrary, he relied heavily and publicly on several Jewish advisers, such as Roy Cohn and David Schine. The evidence of surveys further indicates that McCarthy's supporters were not any more anti-Semitic than his opponents.

Suggestions for Further Reading

The *Congressional Quarterly*'s *Congress and the Nation, 1945-1964: A Review of Government and Politics, the Postwar Years* (Washington, 1965) is an invaluable source of information on the McCarthy era. Two liberal interpretations of the period are lively and provocative: Eric F. Goldman, *The Crucial Decade—And After: America, 1945-1960* (New York, 1961) and Herbert Agar, *The Price of Power: America Since 1945* (Chicago, 1957). The perimeters of McCarthyism are discussed in detail in David Caute, *The Great Fear: The Anti-Communist Purge Under Truman And Eisenhower* (New York, 1978) a study marred by its leftist slant. See also Thomas C. Reeves, *Freedom and the Foundation: The Fund for the Republic in the Era of McCarthyism* (New York, 1969), the story of a controversial tax-exempt foundation designed, in part, to deal with civil liberties. Other helpful introductions include Donald J. Kemper, *Decade of* Fear: Senator Hennings and Civil Liberties (Columbia, Missouri, 1965); Ralph B. Levering, *The Cold War, 1945-1972* (Arlington Heights, Illinois, 1982); and Daniel Yergin, *Shattered Peace: The Origins of the Cold War and the National Security State* (Boston, 1978). For more breadth, see Michael Parenti, *The Anti-Communist Impulse* (New York, 1969); David Brion Davis, *The Fear Of Conspiracy: Images of Un-American Subversion From the Revolution to the Present* (Ithaca, New York, 1971); Arthur M. Schlesinger, Jr., *The Imperial Presidency* (Boston, 1973); and Michael W. Miles, *The Odyssey of the American Right* (New York 1980). Dalton Trumbo, *The Time of the Toad: A Study of Inquisition in America* (New York 1972) is a zesty account from the Far Left.

There is a large body of literature on civil liberties in the postwar period, though much of it is polemical and must be handled with care. The standard works include Milton R. Konvitz, *Expanding Liberties: Freedom's Gains in Postwar America* (New York, 1966); Robert E. Cushman, *Civil Liberties in the United States* (Ithaca, New York, 1956); John H. Schaar, *Loyalty in America* (Berkeley, 1957); and John W. Caughey, *In Clear and Present Danger: The Crucial State of Our Freedoms* (Chicago, 1958). Narrower, but no less valuable, works include Eleanor Bontecou, *The Federal Loyalty-Security Program* (Ithaca, New York, 1953); John Lord O'Brian, *National Security and Individual Freedom* (Cambridge, Mass., 1955); and Ralph S. Brown, *Loyalty and Security Employment Tests in the United States* (New Haven, Connecticut, 1958). Samuel A. Stouffer, *Communism, Conformity, and Civil Liberties: A Cross-section of the Nation Speaks Its Mind* (New York, 1955) contains revealing public opinion polls. For solid, more recent studies, see David P. Gardner, *The California Oath Controversy* (Berkeley and Los Angeles, 1967); Jane Sanders, *Cold War on the Campus* (Seattle, 1979); Stanley Kutler, *The American Inquisition: Justice and Injustice in the Cold War* (New York, 1982); Ronald Radash and Joyce Milton, *The Rosenberg File: A Search for the Truth* (New York, 1983); Don E. Carleton, *Red Scare: Right-wing Hysteria, Fifties Fanaticism, and Their Legacy in*

Texas (Austin, Texas, 1985); and Ellen W. Schrecker, *No Ivory Tower: Mc-Carthyism and the Universities* (New York, 1986), a brilliant piece of research damaged by its left-wing bias.

Congressional investigations of subversive activities are discussed, though frequently with passion, in Robert K. Carr, *The House Committee on Un-American Activities, 1945-1950* (Ithaca, New York, 1952); Telford Taylor, *Grand Inquest: The Story of Congressional Investigations* (New York, 1955); Alan Barth, *Government By Investigation* (New York, 1955); Frank J. Donner, *The Un-Americans* (New York, 1961); and Walter Goodman, *The Committee: The Extraordinary Career of the House Committee on Un-American Activities* (New York, 1968). Eric Bentley, ed., *Thirty Years of Treason: Excerpts From Hearings Before the House Committee on Un-American Activities, 1938-1968* (New York, 1971) is valuable. William F. Buckley, Jr. and the editors of *National Review, The Committee And Its Critics: a Calm Review of the House Un-American Activities Committee* (New York, 1962) is a right-wing defense of HUAC. Walter Gellhorn, ed., *The States and Subversion* (Ithaca, New York, 1952) is solid and instructive concerning investigations on the state level.

Alistair Cooke's *A Generation on Trial* (New York, 1950) is a rather dry but intelligent interpretation of the Alger Hiss case. Allan Weinstein, *Perjury: The Hiss-Chambers Case* (New York, 1979) is the best account to date and concludes that Hiss was guilty. Athan Theoharis, ed., *Beyond The Hiss Case: The FBI, Congress, and the Cold War* (Philadelphia, 1982) contains fiery left-wing articles. Hiss defends himself in Alger Hiss, *In the Court of Public Opinion* (New York, 1957). Whittaker Chambers, *Witness* (New York, 1952), by Hiss's accuser, is a work of seminal importance to many conservatives. Harvey Matusow *False Witness* (New York 1955) contains the confessions of a sleazy informer helpful to McCarthy. Herbert L. Packer, *Ex-Communist Witnesses: Four Studies in Fact Finding* (Stanford, California, 1962) is a thoughtful study of informers. See also Victor S. Navasky, *Naming Names* (New York, 1980).

Earl Latham, *The Communist Controversy in Washington From the New Deal to McCarthy* (Cambridge, Massachusetts, 1966) is a brilliant and underrated examination of charges of Communist infiltration of the federal government. Sound studies of American Communism include Theodore Draper, *The Roots of American Communism* (New York, 1957); *American Communism and Soviet Russia* (New York, 1960); David Shannon, *The Decline of American Communism* (New York, 1959); Nathan Glazer, *The Social Basis of American Communism* (New York, 1961); Robert W. Iversen, *The Communists and the Schools* (New York, 1959); and Ralph Lord Roy, *Communism and the Churches* (New York, 1960). Irving Howe and Lewis Coser, *The American Communist Party* (Boston, 1957) and Joseph Starobin, *American Communism in Crisis, 1943-1957* (Cambridge, Massachusetts, 1972) are useful though somewhat slanted. Michal R. Belknap, *Cold War Political Justice: The Smith Act, the Communist Party, and American Civil Liberties* (Westport,

Connecticut, 1977) contains numerous insights despite its partisanship. William L. O'Neill, *A Better World: The Great Schism: Stalinism and the American Intellectuals* (New York, 1982) is excellent. The Fund for the Republic's *Bibliography on the Communist Problem in the United States* (New York, 1955) is a first-rate guide through a great mass of material. See also Joel Seidman, *Communism in the United States: A Bibliography* (Ithaca, New York, 1969).

The standard biography of Senator McCarthy is Thomas C. Reeves, *The Life and Times of Joe McCarthy: A Biography* (New York, 1982). Also useful are Robert Griffith, *The Politics of Fear: Joseph R. McCarthy and the Senate* (Lexington, Kentucky, 1970); and Michael O'Brien, *McCarthy and McCarthyism in Wisconsin* (Columbia, Missouri, 1980). Richard Rovere's popular *Senator Joe McCarthy* (New York, is beautifully written and perceptive but is largely impressionistic and often misleading. Rovere takes the position that McCarthy was a gifted demagogue, a view put forth earlier by Reinhard H. Luthin in *American Demagogues* (Boston, 1954). James Rorty and Moshe Decter, in *McCarthy and the Communists* (Boston, 1954), argue that the Wisconsin Senator actually, however unintentionally, assisted Communist aims. Fred J. Cook, *The Nightmare Decade: The Life and Times of Senator Joe McCarthy* (New York, 1971) and Lately Thomas, *When Even Angels Wept: The Senator Joseph McCarthy Affair—A Story Without a Hero* (New York, 1973) are anti-McCarthy tirades of little value. Michael Straight, *Trial by Television* (Boston, 1954) interprets the Army-McCarthy hearings. Donald J. Crosby's *God, Church, and Flag: Senator Joseph R. McCarthy and the Catholic Church, 1950-1957* attempts with some success to challenge the belief in a close association between McCarthy and the Roman Catholic clergy and laity. Robert Griffith and Athan Theoharis, eds., *The Specter: Original Essays on the Cold War and the Origins of McCarthyism* (New York, contains a number of first-rate studies of McCarthy and the Second Red Scare. The essays by Ronald Lora, "A View From the Right: Conservative Intellectuals, the Cold War, and McCarthy," and Peter H. Irons, "American Business and the Origins of McCarthyism" are particularly helpful. Foremost among the friendly interpretations of McCarthy's career are *McCarthy and His Enemies: The Record and Its Meaning* (Chicago, 1954) by William F. Buckley, Jr. and L. Brent Bozell; and Roy Cohn, *McCarthy* (New York, 1968) [republished in 1977 under the title *McCarthy: The Answer to "Tail Gunner Joe."*] Medford Evans, *The Assassination of Joe McCarthy* (Boston 1970) is a bizarre exercise in exaltation by a member of the John Birch Society. William Schlamm, "Across McCarthy's Grave," *National Review*, 2 (May, 18, 1957) strikes a similar tone and was the favorite eulogy of McCarthy's widow. For a Marxist interpretation, drawing parallels between McCarthy and Hitler, see Leo B. Huberman and Paul M. Sweezy, "The Roots and Prospects of McCarthyism," *Monthly Review*, 8 (January, 1954). See also Nicholas Von Hoffman, *Citizen Cohn* (New York, 1988) and Sidney Zion, ed., *The Autobiography of Roy Cohn* (Secaucus, New Jersey, 1988), popular treatments of McCarthy's principal lieutenant.

Several who clashed with McCarthy put their impressions in print. Owen Lattimore, *Ordeal by Slander* (Boston, 1950) is an eloquent and not entirely convincing description of the warfare between the Senator and the controversial scholar. James A. Wechsler, *Age of Suspicion* (New York, 1953) tells of McCarthy's efforts to stifle attacks from a liberal critic. Leroy Gore, *Joe Must Go* (New York, 1954) is the fascinating account of a rural Wisconsin newspaper editor's attempt to recall Senator McCarthy. The recollections of a member of the McCarthy Committee are in Charles Potter, *Days of Shame* (New York, 1965). Arthur V. Watkins, *Enough Rope* (Englewood Cliffs, New Jersey, 1969) presents the Utah Senator's story of McCarthy's censure. Ralph E. Flanders, *Senator from Vermont* (New York, 1961) is by one of McCarthy's most outspoken critics. Margaret Chase Smith, *Declaration of Conscience* (New York, 1972) is by another Senator who challenged McCarthy. Edward Bennet Williams, *One Man's Freedom* (New York, 1962) contains brief, superficial recollections by McCarthy's attorney during the censure proceedings. There are also interesting memories of McCarthy in Earl Mazo, *Richard Nixon, A Political and Personal Portrait* (New York, 1959); Sidney Hyman, *The Lives of William Benton* (Chicago, 1969); Clinton P. Anderson, *Outsider In the Senate: Senator Clinton Anderson's Memoirs* (New York, 1970); Paul H. Douglas, *In The Fullness of Time, The Memoirs of Paul H. Douglas* (New York, 1971); Walter Trohan, *Political Animals, Memoirs of a Sentimental Cynic* (New York, 1975); Ovid Demaris, ed., *The Director, An Oral Biography of J. Edgar Hoover* (New York, 1975); Jack Anderson and James Boyd, *Confessions of a Muckraker, The Inside Story of Life in Washington during the Truman, Eisenhower, Kennedy and Johnson Years* (New York, 1979); Richard Nixon, *RN: The Memoirs of Richard Nixon, Volume One* (New York, 1979); Barry Goldwater, *With No Apologies* (New York, 1979); William C. Sullivan, *The Bureau: My Thirty Years in Hoover's FBI* (New York, 1979); and Merle Miller, *Lyndon, An Oral Biography* (New York, 1980). See also the several revealing tributes from Congressional colleagues in *Memorial Services Held in the Senate and House of Representatives of the United States, Together with Remarks Presented in Eulogy of Joseph Raymond McCarthy Late a Senator From Wisconsin* (Washington, 1957). The standard study of McCarthy's enemies is Richard M. Fried's excellent *Men Against McCarthy* (New York, 1976).

Athan Theoharis, *Seeds of Repression: Harry S. Truman and the Origins of McCarthyism* (Chicago, 1971), as the selection indicates, argues that "The inconsistencies between the Truman administration's go-for-broke rhetoric and its cautious military response in Korea paved the way for the success of Joseph McCarthy and his followers." This same anti-liberal approach may be seen in John Steinke and James Weinstein, "McCarthy and the Liberals," *Studies on the Left*, 2 (1962); Richard M. Freeland, *The Truman Doctrine and the Origins of McCarthyism: Foreign Policy, Domestic Politics, and Internal Security, 1946-1948* (New York, 1972); and Mary Sperling McAuliffe, *Crisis on the Left: Cold War Politics and American Liberals, 1947-1954* (Amherst, Massachusetts, 1978). On the other hand, Alan D.

Harper, *The Politics of Loyalty: The White House and the Communist Issue, 1946-1952* (Westport, Connecticut, 1969) carefully depicts the political atmosphere which prompted the Truman loyalty program and sees the President as a defender of civil liberties. Truman is also treated sympathetically in Alonzo L. Hamby, *Beyond the New Deal: Harry S. Truman and American Liberalism* (New York, 1973), one of our most impressive studies of postwar America. Truman's own appraisal of his motives and actions is in his *Years of Trial and Hope* (New York, 1956). A pertinent selection of documents is in Barton J. Bernstein and Allen J. Matusow, eds., *The Truman Administration: A Documentary History* (New York, 1966). William C. Berman's "Civil Rights and Civil Liberties" in Richard S. Kirkendall, ed., *The Truman Period As a Research Field* (Columbia, Missouri, 1967) is a good bibliographical essay and contends that the Truman administration "inadvertently let loose the Yahoos" and was "victimized by its own efforts to contain them." Francis H. Thompson, *The Frustration Of Politics: Truman, Congress and the Loyalty Issue, 1945-1953* (Cranbury, New Jersey, 1979) is a largely unsuccessful effort to grapple with the general topic. Excellent recent studies include Robert H. Ferrell, *Harry S. Truman and the Modern American Presidency* (Boston, 1983); and Donald R. McCoy, *The Presidency of Harry S. Truman* (Lawrence, Kansas, 1984).

For important studies of the Korean War and its relationship to McCarthyism, see John W. Spanier, *The Truman-MacArthur Controversy and the Korean War* (New York, 1965); and Ronald J. Caridi, *The Korean War and American Politics: The Republican Party as a Case Study* (Philadelphia, 1968). On McCarthyism and the China question, see John S. Service, *The Amerasia Papers: Some Problems in the History of U.S.-China Relations* (Berkeley, California, 1971); John N. Thomas, *The Institute of Pacific Relations, Asian Scholars and American Politics* (Seattle, 1974); E.J. Kahn, Jr., *The China Hands: America's Foreign Service Officers and What Befell Them* (New York, 1975); Gary May, *China Scapegoat: The Diplomatic Ordeal of John Carter Vincent* (New York, 1979); and Joseph Keeley, *The China Lobby Man: The Story of Alfred Kohlberg* (New Rochelle, New York, 1969), a view from the Far Right.

President Eisenhower briefly discusses his disdain for McCarthy in *The White House Years: Mandate for Change, 1953-1956* (New York, 1963). Sherman Adams, *Firsthand Report, The Story of the Eisenhower Administration* (New York, 1961) adds little. Charles E. Potter's *Days of Shame* recounts conversations with Eisenhower during the Army-McCarthy hearings. Emmet John Hughes, *The Ordeal of Power: A Political Memoir of the Eisenhower Years* (New York, 1963) contains a scathing indictment of the administration's timidity toward McCarthy and a few revealing glimpses of Richard Nixon. See also Robert Cutler *No Time for Rest* (Boston, 1965); Charles E. Bohlen, *Witness to History, 1929-1969* (New York, 1973); and Eleanor Lansing Dulles, "Footnote to History: A Day in the Life of Senator Joe McCarthy," *World Affairs*, 143 (Fall, 1980). In recent years it has become fashionable to give Eisenhower the credit for deflating McCarthy. This unconvincing thesis is pursued in Blanche Cook, *The Declassified Eisenhower* (Garden City, New York, 1981) and Fred I. Greenstein, *The Hidden-Hand Presidency: Eisenhower as Leader* (New York, 1982). See Thomas C. Reeves, "The Myth of Eisenhower's 'Hidden Hand' and the Downfall of Senator Joe McCarthy," *The Valley Forge Journal*, III (1986). For two first-rate studies of Eisenhower, see Robert Divine, *Eisenhower and the Cold War* (New York, 1981) and Stephen E. Ambrose, *Eisenhower, The President* (New York, 1984).

Students of the "status anxiety" explanations for the rise of McCarthyism should read the articles and sources cited in Daniel Bell, ed., *The New American Right* (New York, 1955), and its revised edition, *The Radical Right* (New York, 1963). There are also valuable reflections in Richard Hofstadter, *The Paranoid Style in American Politics and Other Essays* (New York, 1965). In *The Politics of Unreason: Right-Wing Extremism in America, 1790-1970* (New York, 1970) by Seymour Martin Lipset and Earl Raab, the general hypothesis is applied to the whole of United States history. Nelson W. Polsby, "Toward an Explanation of McCarthyism," *Political Studies*, III (1960) attacks the theory with statistics and hard arguments. C. Vann Woodward, "The Populist Heritage and the Intellectual," *American Scholar*, XXIX (Winter, 1959-1960) counters effectively the tendency to link Populism with McCarthyism. Michael Paul Rogin, *The Intellectuals and McCarthy: The Radical Specter* (Cambridge, Massachusetts, 1967) disproves the assertion that McCarthyism grew out of agrarian radicalism and attributes it to a traditional conservative heritage. For an analysis of the status theories, see Thomas C. Reeves, "McCarthyism: Interpretations Since Hofstadter," *The Wisconsin Magazine of History*, 60 (1976). The best study of modern conservatism is George H. Nash, *The Conservative Intellectual Movement in America, Since 1945* (New York, 1976). *The Rise of the Right* (New York, 1984), by conservative leader William A. Rusher, carefully sidesteps McCarthy and his "ism" but has much to say about the anti-Communist outlook of the postwar Right.

Several studies within the extensive literature on McCarthyism and the mass media are of special value: John Cogley, *Report on Blacklisting*, 2 vols. (New York, 1956); John Henry Faulk, *Fear On Trial* (New York, 1964); Robert Vaughn, *Only Victims: A Study of Show Business Blacklisting* (New York, 1972); Larry Ceplair and Steven Englund, *The Inquisition in Hollywood: Politics in the Film Community, 1930-1960* (Garden City, New York, 1980); Victor Nevasky, *Naming Names* (New York, 1980); Edwin R. Bayley, *Joe McCarthy and the Press* (Madison, Wisconsin, 1981). See also Lillian Hellman, *Scoundrel Time* (New York, 1976) the fascinating recollections of a fellow-traveler.

Students interesting in reading primary sources in this field may feel overwhelmed by the volume and variety available. Here are some suggestions. From the Far Right see Robert Stripling, *The Red Plot Against America* (New York 1949); Joseph R. McCarthy, *America's Retreat from Victory, The Story of George Catlett Marshall* (New York, 1951); and *McCarthyism: The Fight for America* (New York, 1952);

Vincent Hartnett, "New York's Great Red Way," *American Mercury*, 76 (June, 1953); Herbert Philbrick, *I Led 3 Lives* (New York, 1953); Howard Rushmore, "Robert Morris," *American Mercury*, 76 (March-April, 1953); Herbert Brownell, Jr., "Reds Are Trying To Wreck Informant System of FBI," *U.S. News and World Report*, 38 (April 1, 1955); James D. Bales, ed., *J. Edgar Hoover Speaks* (Nutley, New Jersey, 1970). For examples of polemics from the Far Left, see Howard Fast, "We Have Kept Faith," *Masses and Mainstream*, 3 (July, 1950); Michael Harrington, "The American Committee for Cultural Freedom," *Dissent*, 2 (Spring, 1953); Herbert Aptheker, "Communism and Truth," *Masses and Mainstream*, 6 (February, 1953); G. Bromley Oxnam, *I Protest* (New York, 1954); Corliss Lamont, "Conform—Or Lose Your Job," *Monthly Review*, 7 (February, 1956); Jay G. Sykes, "Post-McCarthy Delusions of Liberty," *Monthly Review*, 7 (February, 1956). Useful materials from the more-or-less mainstream would include Leonard Engel, "Fear in Our Laboratories," *The Nation*, 166 (January 17, 1948); Henry Steele Commager, "Red-Baiting in the Colleges," *New Republic*, 121 (July 25, 1949); Carey McWilliams, *Witch Hunt—The Revival of Heresy* (Boston, 1950); Ellen Knauff, *The Ellen Knauff Story* (New York, 1952); Sidney Hook, *Heresy, Yes—Conspiracy, No* (New York, 1953); Marie Jahoda, "Morale in the Federal Civil Service," *Annals of the American Academy of Political and Social Science*, 300 (July, 1955); James Rorty, "The Dossier of Wolf Ladejinsky," *Commentary*, 19 (April, 1955); Scientists Committee on Loyalty and Security, "Fort Monmouth One Year Later," *Bulletin of the Atomic Scientists*, 11 (April, 1955); Murray Kempton, "The Achievement of Harvey Matusow," *The Progressive*, 19 (April, 1955); Ring Lardner, Jr., "My Life on the Blacklist," *Saturday Evening Post*, 234 (October 14, 1961).

For a first-rate bibliography of largely scholarly books and articles on the general field, see John Earl Haynes (ed.), *Communism and Anti-Communism in the United States: An Annotated Guide to Historical Writings* (New York, 1987).